Unit E

Wings and Rockets

Flight and Properties of Air

I WONDER

Science begins with wondering. What do you wonder about when you watch an airplane flying overhead? What questions would you like to ask the pilot of an airplane? Write down your questions, and be ready to share them with the rest of the class.

An early hang glider (1896)

Biplanes on the runway, Cottage Grove, Oregon

The space shuttle *Discovery* takes off.

I PLAN

You may have asked questions like these about flight. Scientists also ask questions. Then they plan ways to find answers to their questions. Now you and your classmates can plan how you will investigate flight.

My Science Log

- What causes wind?

- What lighter-than-air gases help balloons and blimps fly?

- How do kites fly?

- How can air be strong enough to lift an airplane?

- How can rockets fly, even though there is no air in space?

With Your Class

Plan how your class will use the activities and readings in the **I Investigate** part of this unit.

On Your Own

There are many ways to learn about flight. Following are some things you can do to explore flight on your own or with some classmates. Some explorations may take longer than others. Look over the suggestions and choose . . .

- **Projects to Do**
- **People to Contact**
- **Books to Read**

PROJECTS TO DO

ILLUSTRATED DICTIONARY OF FLIGHT

Work with a small group of classmates. Start by making a list of words you want to include in your dictionary of flight. Alphabetize the words. Then draw a picture to illustrate each word, and write a short explanation of what the word means. Fasten the pages together to make a book, and design a cover for your dictionary.

TIME LINE

Make an illustrated time line about flight. Find or draw a picture about an important event in the history of flight. On your picture, write the year the event took place. Put your

picture with your classmates' pictures. Arrange them all in order by year, and tape them or clip them to a string to make the time line.

MUSEUM EXHIBIT

Organize a museum exhibit about flight for your classroom. Bring in models and toys to show things that fly, such as airplanes, helicopters, kites, and gliders. Bring in flight souvenirs, such as old boarding passes, airline tickets, flight bags, and postcards of airplanes. Write a few sentences on an index card for each of your items. You may want to invite another class to visit your museum exhibit.

PEOPLE TO CONTACT

IN PERSON

To learn more about air travel, talk to people about flights they have taken. Ask them to describe the inside of the airplane. Ask them what they could see out the window.

Talk to some older people about how air travel today is different from air travel years ago.

Talk to a pilot. Ask the pilot some of the questions you wrote in the **I Wonder** part of this unit.

BY TELEPHONE OR MAIL

Many people work in the field of flight. Some of them work for airlines or government agencies. Others work for societies or museums that are interested in flight.

You may write to the following organizations for information.

Here are groups you may write or call.

- National Aeronautics and Space Administration (NASA)
- Students for the Exploration and Development of Space (SEDS)

- American Kitefliers Association
- World Kite Museum and Hall of Fame

BY COMPUTER

Use a computer with a modem to connect to on-line services or bulletin boards. You can look for information on flight. You can also ask if there are events or exhibits about flight that are near you.

BOOKS TO READ

Why Can't I Fly?

by Ken Brown (Doubleday, 1990). An ostrich is a bird with wings and feathers, but it cannot fly. This is a story of one ostrich that dreams of flying and wants to prove to his friends and to himself that he can. He tries many ways of flying, but each attempt fails. How can his friends help him make his dream come true? Read this book to find out.

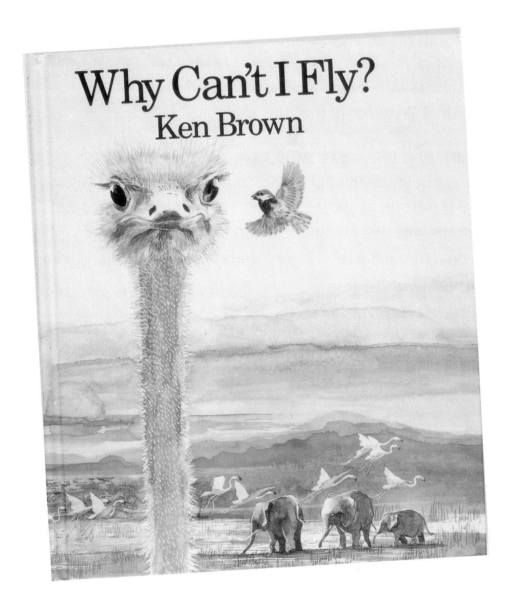

The Air Around Us

by Eleonore Schmid (North-South Books, 1992). Take a deep breath. Every living creature on Earth breathes air. Air is all around us, but we cannot see, smell, or feel it. In this book, you'll find out all about air. It is strong. Wind can blow down trees and lift and carry heavy things. Air is fast. It can race across a field. Air can carry sound. You can hear it whistle through trees or around rocks.

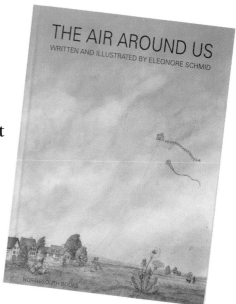

More Books to Read

Dream Planes

by Thomas G. Gunning (Macmillan, 1992). Have you ever seen a car that can fly? This book has a picture of one and explains how it will work. The book also tells about other kinds of airplanes planned for the future.

Flight

by Hilary Devonshire (Franklin Watts, 1992). This book is packed with illustrations and directions for experiments to do and for fun things to make and decorate. Choices include gliders, hot-air balloons, parachutes, a flying seagull, and paper airplanes you can control.

Lindbergh

by Chris L. Demarest (Crown, 1993). Charles Lindbergh was the first pilot to fly an airplane solo and nonstop across the Atlantic Ocean. This beautifully illustrated book describes Lindbergh's childhood in Minnesota. It also tells how he became a pilot, and it follows his heroic flight.

Voyager to the Planets

by Necia H. Apfel (Clarion, 1991), Outstanding Science Trade Book. This story of the *Voyager* mission includes wonderful photographs that were sent back to Earth. These pictures show us the beauty of the outer planets Jupiter, Saturn, Uranus, and Neptune.

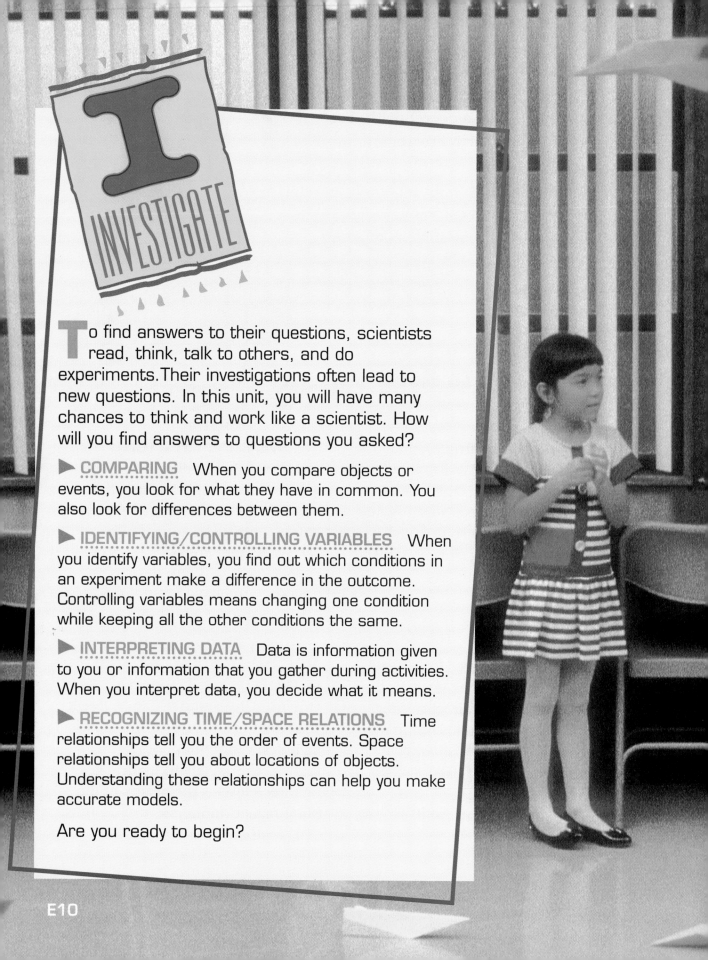

INVESTIGATE

To find answers to their questions, scientists read, think, talk to others, and do experiments. Their investigations often lead to new questions. In this unit, you will have many chances to think and work like a scientist. How will you find answers to questions you asked?

▶ COMPARING When you compare objects or events, you look for what they have in common. You also look for differences between them.

▶ IDENTIFYING/CONTROLLING VARIABLES When you identify variables, you find out which conditions in an experiment make a difference in the outcome. Controlling variables means changing one condition while keeping all the other conditions the same.

▶ INTERPRETING DATA Data is information given to you or information that you gather during activities. When you interpret data, you decide what it means.

▶ RECOGNIZING TIME/SPACE RELATIONS Time relationships tell you the order of events. Space relationships tell you about locations of objects. Understanding these relationships can help you make accurate models.

Are you ready to begin?

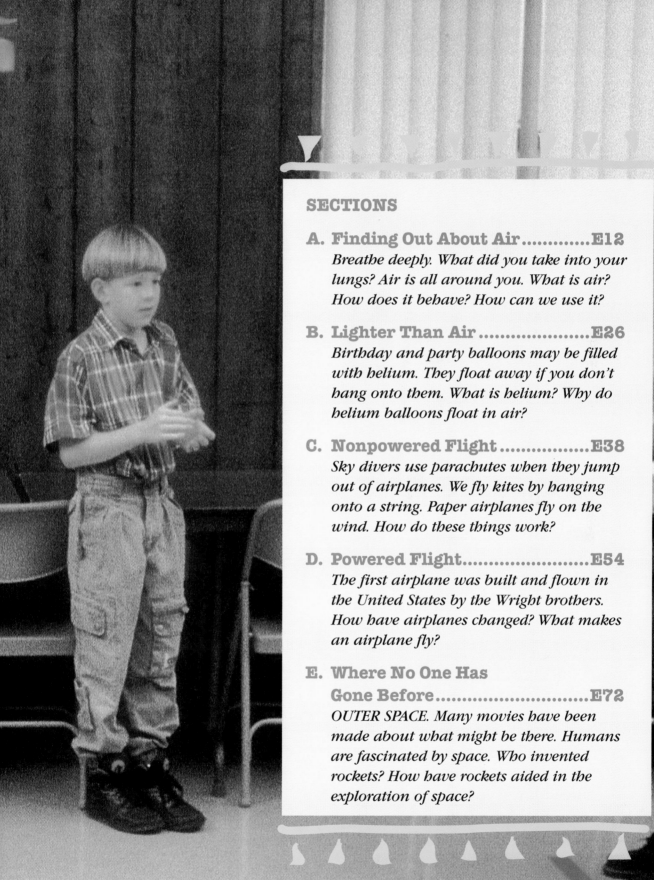

SECTIONS

SECTION A
Finding Out About Air

The airplane sits at the end of a runway. Its engines roar. It races down the runway and takes off into the air. The airplane uses its engines and wings to fly, but does it use the air to fly? Do airplanes—as well as balloons, helicopters, and birds—need air to fly? What is air? In this section, you will have a chance to explore what air is and how it moves.

Can you see the air? Can you feel it? Can you weigh it? Keep careful notes in your Science Log as you work through the following investigations.

1 IT'S A GAS

Look at your desk. If you observe it carefully, you can describe it to someone else. Suppose you needed to describe air to someone. How would you do it?

ACTIVITY

Room for Air

You know air fills things like balloons, but does it fill objects that aren't blown up? Try this activity to find out.

MATERIALS
- apron
- clear plastic jar
- plastic funnel
- clay
- water
- measuring cup
- red food coloring
- spoon
- bowl
- pencil
- Science Log data sheet

DO THIS

1. **CAUTION: Put on an apron, and leave it on for this activity.** Place the funnel in the jar. Mold the clay around the top of the jar to hold the funnel in place. Make sure there are no holes for air to go through.

2. Put five drops of food coloring into a cup of water. Stir.

3. Pour the water into the funnel slowly.

4. With the funnel still in the bottle, turn the bottle upside down. What happens?

5. Hold the bottle over a bowl or a sink. Use a pencil to poke a hole through the clay. What happens now?

THINK AND WRITE

1. Why do you think the water behaved the way it did?

2. What does this tell you about air?

ⒶⒸⓉⒾⓋⒾⓉⓎ

Heavy as Air

Is air heavy? You can find out by trying this activity.

DO THIS

❶ Measure the wood to find the center of its length. Draw a line across the center.

❷ Stick a thumbtack into each side of the wood on the line.

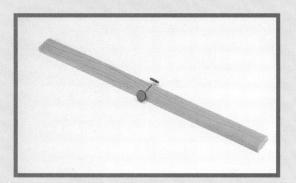

❸ Tie the string around the center of the rubber band. The rubber band should have two loops.

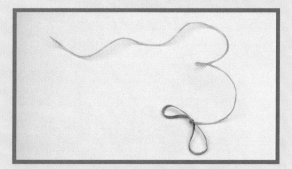

❹ Put a loop of the rubber band around each thumbtack.

❺ Hold up the wood by the end of the string. The wood should balance. If it does not, put a piece of clay on the higher end. The clay should make the wood balance.

MATERIALS

- thin, flat piece of wood (50 cm)
- ruler
- pencil
- 2 thumbtacks
- piece of string (30 cm)
- rubber band
- clay
- 2 identical balloons
- masking tape
- Science Log data sheet

6 Tape an empty balloon to each end of the wood. What happens?

7 Take one balloon off the wood. Blow it up.

8 Tape the blown-up balloon back onto the wood. How does the balance look now?

THINK AND WRITE

1. What did the filled balloon have that the other balloon did not have?

2. What did the air in the balloon do to the balance?

3. What does that tell you about air?

4. **COMPARING** When you investigate, you often compare one thing to another. What did you compare in this activity? What did the comparison tell you?

Looking Back Air seems to be nothing. But air is something. It is matter. Matter is anything that has mass and takes up space. How can you prove that air has mass?

Mass is the amount of matter in a substance. It may be hard to believe that air has mass, because you can't feel its mass. At least you can't feel it in the same way that you feel the mass of your desk.

One reason you know that your desk has mass is that if you try to lift it, your desk feels heavy. Air doesn't feel heavy, but from the activity, you know that air does have mass.

Air Pushes on You

Although air is invisible, it does take up space. It pushes on things, too.

The push caused by air is a force called **air pressure**. Air pressure is a very strong force. It can hold water in a glass that is upside down, and it can make a hot-air balloon rise into the atmosphere.

Air pressure is not the same in every place. It changes with temperature. The particles in warm air move faster than the particles in cold air. In an open container, the faster moving, warm air particles spread out so that there are fewer particles in the container. This makes a certain amount of warm air lighter than the same amount of cold air. The warm air presses on things with less force. So its air pressure is less, or lower. Cold air has more mass than the same amount of warm air. It presses on things with more force. So its air pressure is greater, or higher.

THINK ABOUT IT

The air inside a hot-air balloon is hot, and the air outside it is cold. Where is the air pressure higher?

ACTIVITY

A Lift from Air

Can air lift objects? Try this activity to find out.

DO THIS

1 Tape the bag shut with the straw coming out. Put the bag at the edge of the table.

2 Put the books on top of the bag but not near the straw.

3 Blow up the bag as much as you can. What happens?

THINK AND WRITE

Write a paragraph that explains what you saw.

QUICK CHECK

LESSON 1 REVIEW

1 Write a paragraph that describes air. Include the properties you discovered.

2 What are some of the effects of air pressure?

E17

2 THE WIND

Look out your classroom window at a tree or a flag. Do you see it moving? What makes it move? In the last lesson, you learned about some properties of air. Wind is just moving air. Read what others have said about wind, and then investigate wind by doing the activities.

Wind Poems

Thousands of poems have been written about wind. Here are a few from different parts of the world. Which ones describe the wind you know?

Japanese Poem

by **Buson**

You can see the morning breeze
Blowing the hairs
Of the caterpillar.

Japanese Poem

by **Asayasu**

A breeze stirs at dawn,
shaking a rain of trembling
dewdrops to the grass.

AFRICAN BUSHMAN POEM

The wind was once a man
Who wandered on the earth,
Now he is a bird
Who flies high.

He became a bird who flies,
Who bites our skin:
A bird we feel, a bird we hear
A bird we cannot see.

The wind-bird seeks food,
The wind-bird hunts,
When it has eaten its prey
It flies home again.

When he hunts, the sky rumbles,
The sand flies around;
When he sleeps the sky rests—
And then we sleep, too.

Native American Kiowa Verse

That wind, that wind
Shakes my tipi, shakes my tipi,
And sings a song for me.

Ribbons of Wind

by Deborah Chandra

Clear
ribbons
of
wind
ripple
and swish,
can you
hear them
curl and
twist
among the
leaves?
Great rolls
of windfall
ribbons
rub a
silken
hiss
as they
slip
between
the bushes,
through
the
trees.

THINK ABOUT IT

Compare the ways in which the authors of these poems describe the wind. From each poem, choose a word that describes something the wind does.

Up and Away

You can cause wind to blow right inside your classroom. Try this activity to see what causes the wind.

DO THIS

1 Tape the black paper on a wall just behind the lamp.

2 **CAUTION: Do not breathe the cornstarch.** The lamp must be off. Squeeze a puff of cornstarch above the light bulb. What happens?

3 **CAUTION: Do not touch the light bulb. It can burn you.** Turn the lamp on. Give the bulb 10 minutes to get hot.

4 Squeeze a puff of cornstarch above the light bulb again. What happens to this puff of cornstarch?

5 Draw or write about what happened to each puff of cornstarch.

MATERIALS

- black construction paper
- masking tape
- lamp with its shade removed
- squeezable container of baby powder with cornstarch
- Science Log data sheet

1. How did the cornstarch move over the cold bulb? How did it move over the hot bulb?

2. Why do you think the cornstarch moved the way it did each time?

3. **RECOGNIZING TIME/SPACE RELATIONSHIPS** Recording the amount of time needed for something to happen is often an important thing to do in science activities. In this activity, you waited 10 minutes for the bulb to heat up. Why did you wait? What would have happened if you had tried the activity after waiting for one minute? What would have happened if you had waited for 20 minutes?

What Causes Wind?

Did you ever wonder what makes the wind? Join the crowd! People have wondered about this for thousands of years.

In the activity, a small wind was caused by the heat of the lamp. In the real world, wind is caused by differences in air temperature just above the Earth's surface. Some areas of the Earth's surface get more heat from the sun than others. Some of the heat warms the air above the surface. In these warmer areas, particles of air move faster and spread farther apart. So the air is lighter there, and the air pressure is lower.

The air is cooler above surfaces that aren't as warm. There the particles of air move more slowly. They are closer together. So the air is heavier, and the air pressure is higher.

Air moves from areas of high pressure to areas of low pressure. It's almost like water running down a hill. This air movement is called *wind*.

Along the ground, air in high-pressure areas whooshes toward areas of low pressure. The cooler, heavier air pushes the warmer, lighter air upward. The warmer air cools as it rises. As it cools, the air gets heavier. The cooler air then sinks.

This high-pressure air reaches the ground again. Then it flows along the ground toward the area of warmer, low-pressure air. It gets warmer and rises again. The cycle repeats and repeats.

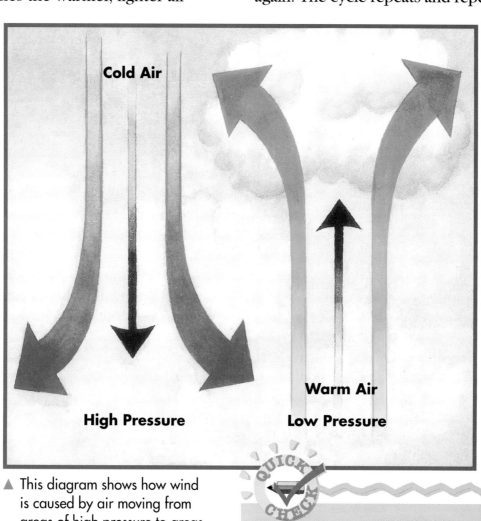

Cold Air

High Pressure

Warm Air

Low Pressure

▲ This diagram shows how wind is caused by air moving from areas of high pressure to areas of low pressure.

QUICK CHECK

LESSON 2 REVIEW

❶ How is the moving air above a heat source like the wind?

❷ What causes wind?

3 THE POWER OF WIND

Daniel Bernoulli was a mathematician who lived about 200 years ago. He studied how wind affects objects. Through his experiments, he learned some very interesting facts about why things fly. You can do similar experiments to find out more about wind and flying.

Air Streams and Air Pressure

The next activities show the effects of air pressure. In each activity, predict what will happen.

ACTIVITY

Have a Ball

DO THIS

1. Tape the string to the ball.

2. Turn on the faucet. Let the water run fast.

3. Hold the string and ball near the stream of running water. Don't let the water touch the ball.

4. Record your observations.

THINK AND WRITE

Write a paragraph that explains what you saw.

MATERIALS
- table-tennis ball
- piece of string (8 cm)
- transparent tape
- sink with a faucet
- Science Log data sheet

E23

The Cans Can

DO THIS

1 Place the cans on their sides. They should be about 3 cm apart.

2 Blow air between the cans through the straw.

MATERIALS

- 2 empty soft-drink cans
- ruler
- drinking straw
- Science Log data sheet

3 Place the cans 2 cm apart. Blow between them through the straw again.

4 Place the cans 1 cm apart. Blow between them one more time.

5 Record your observations.

THINK AND WRITE

1. What happened when you blew between the cans?

2. How did the effect change as you moved the cans closer together?

3. Why do you think the cans acted as they did?

4. **INTERPRETING DATA** When you interpret data, you decide what the data means or how it applies to other situations. Use your data from this activity to explain how the wind might affect things that fly.

LESSON 3 REVIEW

1 What does low air pressure between two objects cause the objects to do?

2 What would happen to two objects if the air pressure between them were high instead of low?

DOUBLE CHECK

SECTION A REVIEW

1. Describe the properties of air that you have learned about.

2. Explain what causes wind.

3. How does the speed of wind affect air pressure?

4. Design a demonstration to show how the speed of wind affects air pressure.

Lighter Than Air

The sun is just starting to rise, and the air is cool and still. You climb into a basket attached to a big, colorful balloon. The balloon strains against the ropes holding it down. Then someone releases the ropes— and up you go. Soon you are so high that the trees below look like dots.

Balloons were among the first flying machines. So were airships such as blimps. What makes it possible for huge balloons to float through the air?

In this section, you can explore the answer to that question and others you may have about lighter-than-air flight. Keep your notes in your Science Log.

▲ **One of the first hot-air balloons**

1 FLOATING IN AIR

Smoke rises. People noticed that long ago. At first they thought that smoke could make things fly. Then people discovered something important. It's not the dark particles in smoke that makes smoke rise. It's something else. What do you think it is?

ACTIVITY

Why Things Float

Rising is the same as floating. Why do things float? Try this activity to find out.

DO THIS

1 Predict which is heavier— water or oil. Write down your prediction.

2 Measure 50 mL of water. Pour it into one of the containers.

3 Measure 50 mL of cooking oil. Pour it into the other container.

4 Put the container of cooking oil on one side of the balance.

5 Put the container of water on the other side of the balance. What happens?

6 Now make another prediction. Which liquid will float on top of the other? Explain your answer. Test your prediction.

THINK AND WRITE

Would oil and water still behave the same way if there were much more oil than water? Explain your answer.

ACTIVITY

Air Takes Up Space

When oil and water are put in the same container, the oil floats on top of the water. This is because the oil is lighter than the water.

Something similar happens with gases. A lighter gas floats in a heavier one. The difference with gases is that when they are put in the same container, they mix together. However, if you can keep them from mixing, the lighter one will float. In fact, you can make a container filled with lighter air that floats in heavier air!

How can you do that? It has to do with how close the air particles are to each other. You can find out one way to change how close together the particles are by trying this activity.

DO THIS

1. Make a chart like the one shown.

2. Blow up the balloon, and tie it shut. Use the marker to draw a line around the middle of the balloon. Measure and record the length of the line.

3. Place the balloon in a freezer overnight. In the morning, measure and record the length of the line again.

MATERIALS
- balloon
- marker
- tape measure
- freezer
- hair dryer
- Science Log data sheet

HOW DOES TEMPERATURE AFFECT AIR IN A BALLOON?	
Condition	Length of Line Around Balloon
Balloon at Room Temperature	
Balloon After It Comes Out of Freezer	
Balloon After It Has Been Warmed Up for 2 Minutes	
Balloon After It Has Been Warmed Up for 4 Minutes	

4 **CAUTION: Do not touch the balloon with the hair dryer.** Gently warm the balloon with the hair dryer. After 2 minutes, measure and record the length of the line. Warm the balloon for another 2 minutes, and measure and record the length of the line.

THINK AND WRITE

1. Describe what happened to the balloon when the air inside became colder and when it became warmer.

2. Explain why you think the balloon changed size.

Hot and Cold

Temperature affects how close together air particles are. When the air is cold, the particles move slowly and are close together. When the air is hot, the particles move quickly and are farther apart.

In warm air, particles are farther apart. ▼

In cold air, particles are closer together. ▼

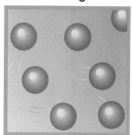

The air particles themselves don't change when the temperature changes.

In a closed container like a balloon or a tire, the container changes size as the air particles move closer together or farther apart. In an open container like a hot-air balloon, some of the heated air escapes. As this happens, there are fewer particles in the same amount of space. So the hot-air balloon becomes lighter.

THINK ABOUT IT

Suppose you fill your bicycle tires on a cold day. A week later, the weather is hot. What should you do to your tires?

ACTIVITY

Modeling a Hot-Air Balloon

You have learned that a certain amount of warm air takes up more space than the same amount of cold air. What happens if you warm up the air in a container so that some of the air can escape?

DO THIS

❶ Set the hair dryer on warm.

❷ **CAUTION: Do not touch the end of the dryer with your hand or the bag.** Ask your partner to hold the plastic bag upside down. Point the dryer into the upside-down bag. Turn the dryer on. Leave it on for a few seconds.

MATERIALS

• small hair dryer with warm and hot settings
• lightweight plastic bag
• Science Log data sheet

3 Turn the dryer off. Tell your partner to let the bag go.

4 Repeat steps 1–3, but set the hair dryer on hot.

5 Record your observations.

THINK AND WRITE

1. What happened to the plastic bag when the dryer was on warm? on hot?

2. What made the bag do what it did? How do you know?

3. Use what you've learned in this activity to explain how balloons full of heated air might fly.

4. **CONTROLLING VARIABLES** Suppose you were baking muffins with your dad. You were going to make two batches, so you decided to try a little experiment. You and your dad wanted to find out what effect baking powder had on the muffins. In the first batch, you left the baking powder out. In the second batch, you added the amount asked for in the recipe.

   In your baking experiment, you changed only one thing—the amount of baking powder. All the other ingredients and amounts stayed the same.

   In a science experiment, the one thing you change is called a *variable*. Everything else in the experiment must stay the same. If you change two variables at once, you won't know which variable was responsible for your results.

   What variable did you test in this activity? What other things in the experiment could be variables?

The Parts of a Hot-Air Balloon

Take a close look at the parts of a hot-air balloon.

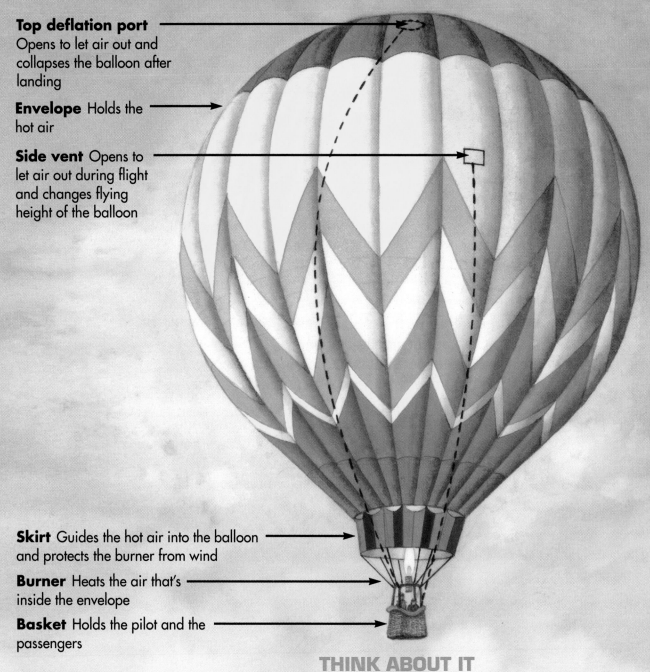

Top deflation port Opens to let air out and collapses the balloon after landing

Envelope Holds the hot air

Side vent Opens to let air out during flight and changes flying height of the balloon

Skirt Guides the hot air into the balloon and protects the burner from wind

Burner Heats the air that's inside the envelope

Basket Holds the pilot and the passengers

THINK ABOUT IT

What could happen to a balloon in flight if its side vent didn't open and close?

How a Hot-Air Balloon Flies

▲ This balloon pilot is using the burner to heat the air inside the envelope.

How does a hot-air balloon pilot make the balloon go up and come down? Read to find out.

To make the balloon go up, the pilot turns the burner on. The burner heats the air inside the envelope. Some air escapes from the opening at the bottom of the envelope. The air in the envelope spreads out, and the balloon rises.

To make the balloon go down, the pilot turns the burner off. The air in the envelope cools. Air outside the balloon rushes in. The balloon becomes heavier and it sinks. The pilot can also let air out of a side vent. This helps the balloon go down.

QUICK CHECK

LESSON 1 REVIEW

❶ How do you know air takes up space?

❷ Why do hot-air balloons float in air?

❸ Why do you think a hot-air balloon might be difficult to control?

2 AIRSHIPS

Hot-air balloons were common in the middle of the 1800s. But the balloons were hard to control. They had no engines. They moved only where the wind blew them. Pilots could not steer them.

Airships solved some of these problems. Airships are egg-shaped balloons. They are filled with gas that is lighter than air.

What Is a Blimp?

You have probably seen a blimp in the sky. What makes a blimp different from a hot-air balloon?

A blimp is a type of airship. Blimps have engines to move them. They also have equipment that helps pilots steer them. A blimp is shaped like the body of an airplane. The long shape helps a blimp move through the air easily.

▲ The first passenger blimps were very fancy. They had formal dining rooms, much like passenger trains of the same time.

▲ These blimps advertise companies and photograph sporting events.

Airships were popular in the late 1800s and early 1900s. They carried passengers in Europe. Like early balloons, the first blimps had hydrogen gas inside. Hydrogen is very light. Air is 15 times as heavy, but hydrogen explodes and burns easily. Many early hydrogen blimps caught fire.

In 1937 a huge German airship called the *Hindenburg* was heading for the United States. It had 97 passengers aboard. The *Hindenburg* exploded over New Jersey, and 36 people were killed. After this disaster, hydrogen gas was no longer used in airships.

Today blimps are filled with helium. You have probably seen helium-filled balloons, so you may know that helium is lighter than air. It is not as light as hydrogen, but it is much safer. Helium does not explode or burn.

Today people still ride in blimps, but the rides are mostly for fun. Blimps are used for other things, though. Sometimes blimps carry cameras so we can see sporting events from the air. These blimps are often used during football games. Blimps are also used to advertise companies. Some advertising blimps are shown here. Do you think this is a good way to advertise a company? Why do you think so?

THINK ABOUT IT

How are blimps different from hot-air balloons?

The Parts of a Blimp

Take a close look at the parts of a blimp. What make a blimp easier to steer than a hot-air balloon?

Envelope This is the outer cover of the blimp. It holds helium, a lighter-than-air gas. Air is seven times heavier than helium.

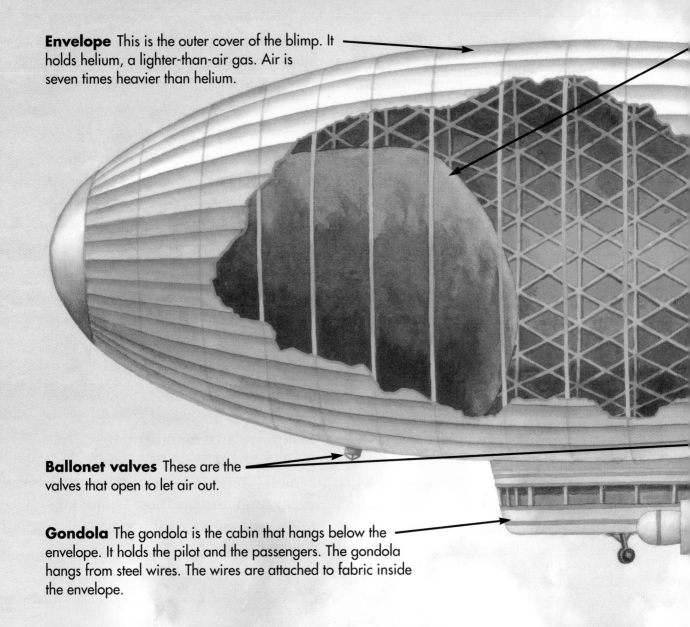

Ballonet valves These are the valves that open to let air out.

Gondola The gondola is the cabin that hangs below the envelope. It holds the pilot and the passengers. The gondola hangs from steel wires. The wires are attached to fabric inside the envelope.

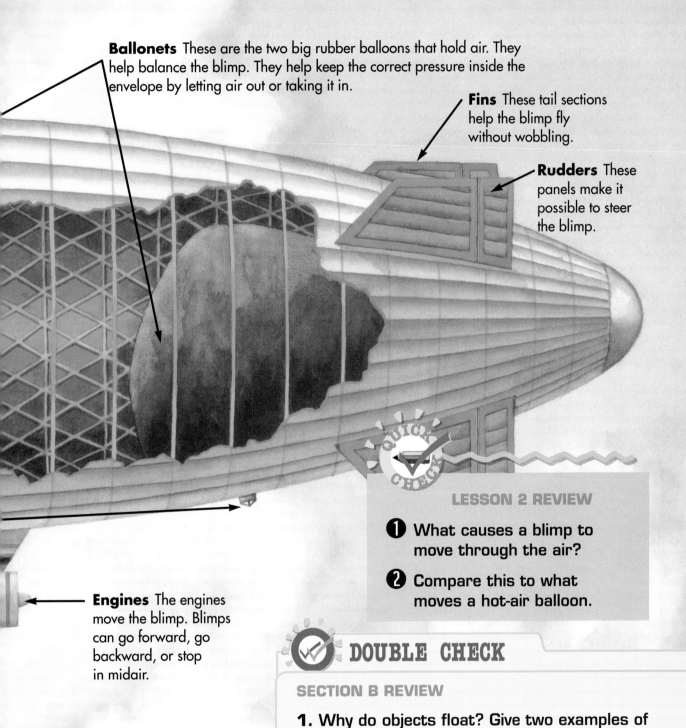

Ballonets These are the two big rubber balloons that hold air. They help balance the blimp. They help keep the correct pressure inside the envelope by letting air out or taking it in.

Fins These tail sections help the blimp fly without wobbling.

Rudders These panels make it possible to steer the blimp.

Engines The engines move the blimp. Blimps can go forward, go backward, or stop in midair.

QUICK CHECK

LESSON 2 REVIEW

❶ What causes a blimp to move through the air?

❷ Compare this to what moves a hot-air balloon.

DOUBLE CHECK

SECTION B REVIEW

1. Why do objects float? Give two examples of things that float.

2. How is what a hot-air balloon uses to float different from what a blimp uses to float?

SECTION C
Nonpowered Flight

Balloons and blimps were among the first flying machines. They fly, but they are big, slow, and hard to control. For these reasons, they can be dangerous.

Long ago, people wondered how they could make a better flying machine. They looked at living things that flew and tried to copy them.

In this section, you will make some simple things that fly: parachutes and kites. You will also make a model of an airplane. Keep careful notes in your Science Log as you investigate.

1 PARACHUTES

Long ago, you might have used a balloon or an airship if you had wanted to fly. What could you have done if you had wanted to fly without a vehicle? You could have used a parachute. Keep reading and find out the secret to making a parachute fly. Then make one yourself.

A Little About Parachutes

Think about what it was like for the first parachute jumper. In 1783 a man climbed to the top of a tower in France. He had something with him that looked like a large umbrella. He opened it, held it over his head, and jumped.

Anything *could* have happened, but the first parachute jumper was lucky. He landed safely.

But people couldn't fly with a parachute in the way they wanted. They just floated to the ground.

The problem was that parachute rides didn't last very long. Balloon rides lasted longer, so people gave up parachutes for balloons.

However, parachutes made a comeback in the early 1900s. Pilots began to use parachutes to escape from airplanes when there was trouble.

Today, parachutes have many uses. Parachutes drop people and supplies into places that are hard to reach. Some people use parachutes to jump, or *sky-dive,* from airplanes for fun.

Some parachutes are shaped like umbrellas. Others are shaped like rectangles. The rectangular parachutes are made of tubes, or cells, arranged side by side. The cells open as the parachute drops. The cells form a wing. The parachute can be steered where the sky diver wants it to go.

▲ This umbrella-shaped parachute allows the jumper to land safely.

◀ This wing-shaped parachute can be steered by the jumper.

THINK ABOUT IT

Why can parachutes be considered safety devices?

Making a Parachute

Now that you know a little about parachutes and how they work, try making one of your own.

MATERIALS
- string (120 cm)
- scissors
- handkerchief
- transparent tape
- stapler
- wooden clothespin
- Science Log data sheet

DO THIS

1 Cut four pieces of string. They must all be the same length, about 30 cm.

2 Tape a string to each corner of the handkerchief. Staple the corners to make the parachute stronger.

3 Pull the loose ends of the four strings together.

4 Tape the four string ends to the wooden clothespin.

5 Throw the parachute into the air. Watch what happens, and record your observations.

THINK AND WRITE

1. What happened to your parachute? Explain what you saw.

2. **RECOGNIZING TIME/SPACE RELATIONSHIPS** After you complete an activity, you sometimes find differences in the time it takes for events to happen. What happened in this activity? How could you cause the experiment to happen more slowly or more quickly?

How a Parachute Works

Here are pictures of a sky diver as she floats to the ground. Study the pictures and the labels to find out more about how a parachute works.

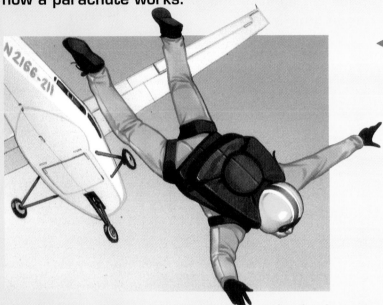

◄ A sky diver jumps when the airplane is about 3,300 meters (10,827 feet) off the ground. The force of gravity pulls her downward until she is falling at about 166 kilometers per hour (103 miles per hour). As she jumps, the sky diver spreads apart her arms and legs. She also arches her back. The shape of her body catches the air and slows her fall.

The sky diver is now 833 meters (2,733 feet) off the ground. She pulls the rip cord. A small parachute pops out of her pack. The rushing wind forces it open. Then the little parachute pulls out the main parachute. ▼

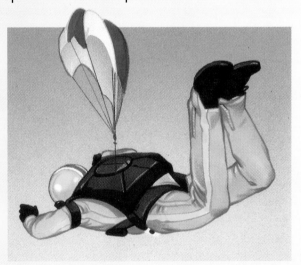

◄ The main parachute opens. Air rushes into the parachute. The force of the air pushing against the parachute slows the sky diver's fall.

◄ The sky diver bends her knees before she lands.

QUICK CHECK

LESSON 1 REVIEW

1 What force causes the sky diver to float slowly to the ground?

2 If there were a hole in the top of the parachute, what might that do to the flight of the sky diver? Explain your answer.

▲ The sky diver's legs take most of the shock of landing. The sky diver rolls when she hits the ground. She unhooks her parachute as soon as she can so the wind will not drag her.

2 KITES

You've heard of flying a kite. Well, how about flying *on* a kite? Explore the history of kites. Then go fly a kite yourself.

The Story of Kites

Kites today are used mostly for fun, but that wasn't always so. Thousands of years ago, the Chinese used kites for many things.

 Early Chinese kites carried messages. Also, Chinese soldiers rode large kites into the sky. From high up, they spied on enemy soldiers.

Chinese fishers used kites to fish in wide lakes and rivers.
They hung hooks with bait from the kites. The hanging kites
could catch fish far from noisy boats that might scare the
fish away.

People who traveled to China wrote about the Chinese kites
they saw. From these writings, people in Europe learned about
kites. In the 1300s, Europeans started to build their own kites.
As these people settled in America, they continued to build
kites there.

▲ Benjamin Franklin flying a kite

Benjamin Franklin was a famous American kite flier. In 1752 Franklin flew a kite in a thunderstorm to test his hypothesis that lightning is a form of electricity. Lightning hit Franklin's kite and a key hanging from it. With his kite and key, Franklin proved that lightning is electricity.

By the late 1800s, many inventors were interested in flight. Most of them tried to fly using parachutes or hot-air balloons. But some were trying to fly on kites.

A British soldier named B. F. S. Baden-Powell was an early kite flier. He wanted to make a kite that would carry a person. Then he could use it to spy on enemy soldiers during battles, just as the Chinese had done thousands of years earlier.

Baden-Powell flew on a kite for the first time in 1894. This kite was really big. It was higher than a three-story building. The kite had a bamboo frame and was covered with canvas. This giant kite lifted Baden-Powell about 3 meters (10 feet) off the ground.

Baden-Powell made a different kind of kite in 1895. He called it the *Levitor.* This kite was actually several kites hooked together. Each kite was 3 meters (10 feet) square.

The *Levitor* rose 33 meters (108 feet) into the air with Baden-Powell aboard. Quite by accident, this strange kite became a useful scientific tool. It helped Guglielmo Marconi, the inventor of the radio. Marconi worked in Europe. He needed to get an antenna up high to pick up a radio signal from Canada, across the Atlantic. A *Levitor* was used to lift the antenna 133 meters (436 feet) into the air to pick up the signal.

Early airplane inventors got some ideas from kites. The Wright brothers, for example, knew a lot about box kites. Their first airplane was much like a box kite with a motor.

In the 1940s, Francis Rogallo made a new kind of kite. The Rogallo wing was shaped like a three-sided parachute. People flew by hanging below Rogallo wings. Today, these wings are called *hang gliders*.

Today, kites are more popular than ever. People fly kites. They also fly *with* kites. Kites have come a long way.

THINK ABOUT IT

Describe three ways to use kites.

Hang gliding allows people to fly with their kites. ▶

ACTIVITY

Go Fly a Kite

Kites have been used for many different purposes through the years. But you can still use them to have fun! Make your own kite and take a flight.

DO THIS

1 On the bag, draw the shapes shown here. Use the measurements shown.

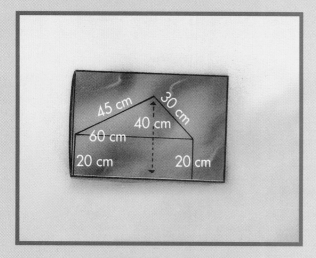

45 cm
30 cm
40 cm
60 cm
20 cm
20 cm

MATERIALS

* large plastic trash bag (61 × 41 cm)
* ruler
* 2 sticks or kite dowels (flat or round, 61 cm × 1.9 cm)
* transparent tape
* white glue
* paper punch
* roll of string
* scissors
* Science Log data sheet

2 Cut out the pattern. Cut through both sides of the bag at once. Unfold the plastic to see the shape of your kite.

3 Glue the dowels to the kite as shown. Let the glue dry. Add tape.

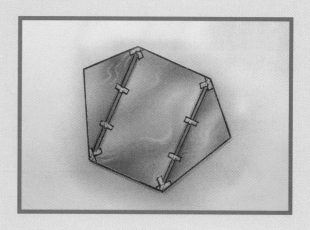

4 Put tape on the points on the right and left flaps of your kite. Punch a hole through each.

5 Cut a 2-m piece of string. Tie one end through one hole. Tie the other end through the other hole. This is the bridle. It should look like the one here.

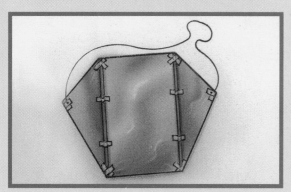

6 Find the center of the bridle. To do this, bring the kite flaps together. Pull up the bridle and find the center. Mark it.

7 Attach the end of the roll of string to the center of the bridle. Your kite is finished. Give it a test to see how well it flies.

8 Draw a picture of your finished kite, and record the details of your test flight.

THINK AND WRITE

1. What kept your kite in the air?

2. What made your kite drop lower in the sky?

3. What could you do to make your kite fly higher?

4. **CONTROLLING VARIABLES** Think carefully about the materials you used to make your kite. Design an experiment that would make the materials the variables. Control the variables, and design a way to test each kite.

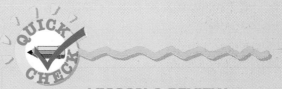

LESSON 2 REVIEW

1 How is the flight of a kite different from the flight of a parachute? How are the flights the same?

2 What happens to a kite when the wind dies down? Explain your answer.

3 PAPER AIRPLANES

Airplanes are the best-known flying machines. What forces help airplanes fly?

ACTIVITY

The Flying Wing

Make a paper wing to learn more about flight.

DO THIS

1. Fold the paper almost in half. The bottom piece should be a little longer than the top.

2. Curve the top of the wing. Tape the edges together and slip the wing over the ruler.

3. **CAUTION: Do not touch the end of the dryer.** Hold up the ruler. Then turn on the dryer. Aim it at the folded side of the wing. What happens?

4. Aim the dryer at other parts of the wing. Now what happens?

THINK AND WRITE

1. What did the wing do? Why?

2. COMPARING In science, you must often compare one thing with another. What did you compare in this activity? What did the comparison tell you?

Looking Back The wing in this activity stands up for the same reason the cans in the activity in Section A moved—differences in air pressure. When air passes over the wing's curved top, it moves faster and, therefore, exerts less pressure than slower-moving air under the wing's straight bottom. With more pressure exerted on the wing from underneath than from the top, the wing is pushed upward.

Up in the Air

Why is it that paper airplanes can fly and you cannot? You weigh more, but a jet plane weighs more than you do and it flies. So there's more to flying than being light in weight.

Flying is all about forces. A **force** is something that pushes or pulls. All airplanes—from paper ones to jumbo jets—use forces to stay in the air.

Toss a paper airplane into the air. There are many forces working on it. Gravity pulls it down. But the power in your arm pushes it ahead. The push is called *thrust*.

When an airplane flies, air pulls against it and slows it down. This pull is called *drag*. Part of the air is also pushing up on the airplane's wings. This upward force is *lift*.

You have to make an airplane carefully if you want to keep it flying. If the wings are too small, for example, there will not be enough lift.

You'll find some flying tips when you turn the page. To see how they work, first you must make a paper airplane.

THINK ABOUT IT

How would the flight of a paper airplane change if there were no drag on it?

Making Paper Airplanes

You have learned about the forces that keep a paper airplane in the air. Now make one yourself.

MATERIALS

- piece of paper (22 cm × 28 cm)
- transparent tape
- 2 or 3 paper clips
- scissors
- Science Log data sheet

DO THIS

1 Fold the paper in half the long way.

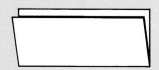

2 Unfold the paper. Now fold two corners to make the nose of the airplane.

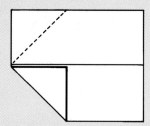

3 Fold both corners again toward the center. Your airplane should look like this.

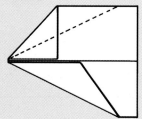

4 Fold the two halves of your airplane together as shown.

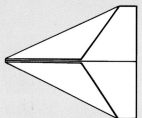

5 Fold one wing down to make the body of the airplane. Turn the airplane over and fold the other wing down.

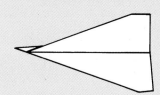

6 To keep the wings together, put a small piece of tape across the top. Now you're ready to fly your airplane!

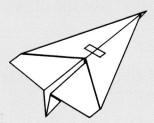

How to Make Your Airplane Fly Farther

Put a paper clip onto the body of your airplane, near the middle. This will help your airplane catch more of the air's lift so it will stay up longer. Experiment to find the best place for the clip. Also, try more than one clip.

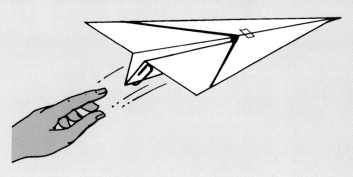

How to Make Your Airplane Turn

Make two cuts on the back edge of each wing as shown. This gives you two wing flaps.

To make your airplane turn right, fold the left wing flap down and the right wing flap up. The air will now push the right wing down and the left wing up. Your airplane will fly to the right. If it doesn't work, try folding the flaps a little less. What would you do to make your airplane go left?

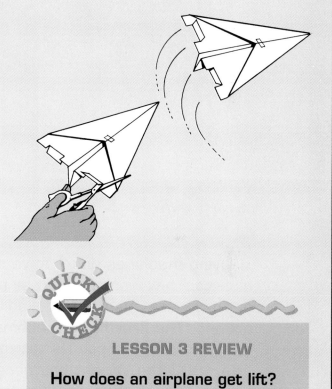

THINK AND WRITE

Design an airplane of your own. Compare the way the two airplanes fly. Then explain how the design changes the way an airplane flies.

QUICK CHECK

LESSON 3 REVIEW

How does an airplane get lift?

DOUBLE CHECK

SECTION C REVIEW

1. Which force is greater on a parachute, lift or gravity? Explain your answer.

2. Kites do not have engines. How do they fly?

E53

Powered Flight

▲ **Bessie Coleman**

Flying machines didn't have engines at first. They were pushed by the wind, or they were pushed or pulled from the ground. The first flying machines with engines were blimps. They were slow and hard to steer.

In 1903 the Wright brothers improved on flying machines with their new airplane. Soon fliers could go farther, faster, and higher than ever before.

What parts of an airplane make it fly? You'll find out in this section. You'll also read about some of the world's great fliers. In your Science Log, keep careful records of all the things you discover.

1 A LOOK AT AIRPLANES

Airplanes are amazing. Some are bigger than a house—and heavier, too. But they still fly!

Wings help keep airplanes in the air. But what force gets airplanes and other flying machines into the air? Investigate this question and others. Then take a closer look at airplanes to find out how all of their parts work together.

World War I biplane ▼

The *Flyer,* the Wright Brothers' plane ▼

B-52 bomber ▶

▲ The Spruce Goose

▲ Stealth bomber

Making a Propeller

Propellers are important to airplanes. Find out more about propellers by making a model propeller.

DO THIS

1 Cut and fold the cardboard to make the stand as shown. Tape together the pieces of the stand.

MATERIALS

- 2 pieces of cardboard (22 × 28 cm)
- scissors
- transparent tape
- 2 paper clips
- rubber band
- Science Log data sheet

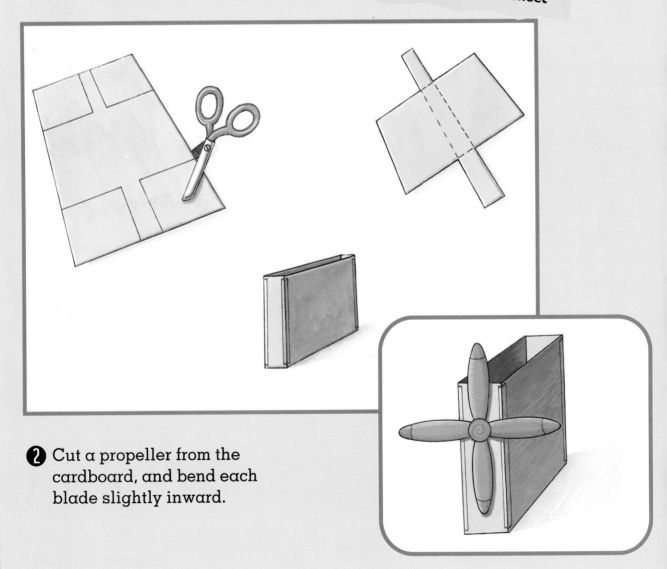

2 Cut a propeller from the cardboard, and bend each blade slightly inward.

❸ CAUTION: Be careful with the paper clips. They may be sharp. Bend the paper clips so they form an "L" shape. Put one paper clip through the center of the propeller. Tape it to the propeller. Push the other paper clip through the back of the stand. Tape it into place, too.

❹ Hold the propeller (with its hook) in front of the stand. Its hook should be right next to the hook in the stand. Put the rubber band over the propeller's hook. Put the other end over the stand's hook.

❺ Now wind the propeller with your finger. Do this until the rubber band is twisted tightly. Put the stand on a flat surface. Let the propeller go. What happens?

THINK AND WRITE

Did your propeller produce thrust? How can you tell?

The Parts of an Airplane

In 1903, the Wright brothers made the first successful powered airplane flight. The airplane was called the *Flyer*. It flew 3 meters (10 feet) into the air and 40 meters (131 feet) across the sands of Kitty Hawk, North Carolina. Then it landed.

A lot has changed since 1903. The *Flyer* was tiny and slow. Today there are huge airplanes that carry hundreds of people. Airplanes can fly very fast and can cross the ocean in just a few hours.

Many airplanes now use jet engines instead of propellers for power. But the other basic parts of the airplane are the same as in the past.

Ailerons The ailerons (AY luh rahnz) on the wings move up and down. They make the wings dip when the airplane turns. This is called a *roll*. One aileron goes up and the other goes down to make the airplane roll. These ailerons are like the ones you put on your paper airplane in the last section.

Propeller The propeller provides the thrust to pull the airplane forward. The blades of the propeller are shaped like wings. Each blade is curved on one side and flat on the other. This shape causes air pressure to be higher behind the propeller. So the propeller pulls the airplane forward. Some airplanes have propellers on their wings.

Control Stick The pilot pushes the control stick forward to make the airplane dive and pulls it backward to make the airplane climb. The pilot moves the control stick from side to side to make the airplane turn.

Rudder The rudder is a flap on the tail. It moves to turn the airplane. To go left or right, the airplane must turn *and* roll. The pilot uses both the rudder and the ailerons to turn.

Elevators The elevators are flaps in the tail section that make the airplane climb (go up) or dive (go down). When the elevators go up, the tail drops and the airplane climbs. When the elevators go down, the tail rises and the airplane dives.

Pedals The pilot presses on the pedals to turn the airplane left or right.

Wings The wings provide lift for the airplane. Wings are curved on top. Air moving over the wings travels farther than air moving under them. The air on top spreads out more, so it has lower air pressure. Higher air pressure under each wing pushes the wing upward.

LESSON 1 REVIEW

❶ Would a propeller help a paper airplane fly? Why or why not?

❷ What would happen to an airplane if it were in the air and forward movement stopped? Explain your answer.

E59

2 HELICOPTERS

A helicopter is another kind of flying machine. It can fly forward and turn, much like a regular airplane. But it can also fly backward and straight up and down. Think about how a helicopter looks different from an airplane. How can the differences allow a helicopter to fly straight up and down?

▲ This helicopter is used to rescue injured people.

▲ This small plane uses a propeller to help it fly.

ACTIVITY

Make a Paper Rotor

A rotor is the big propeller on top of a helicopter. Try making a model of a rotor to see how it works.

DO THIS

1. Cut a 3-cm strip from one long side of the typing paper.

MATERIALS

- sheet of heavy typing paper (22 x 28 cm)
- scissors
- paper clip
- Science Log data sheet

❷ Fold the paper strip in half along its length. Fold the strip three times along its bottom edge.

❸ Cut along the long fold, from the top. Make your cut 10 cm long.

❹ Add a paper clip to the bottom of the rotor. The extra weight will make it work better.

❺ Hold your rotor at shoulder height. Drop it. What happens?

❻ Make a drawing to show the movement of the paper rotor.

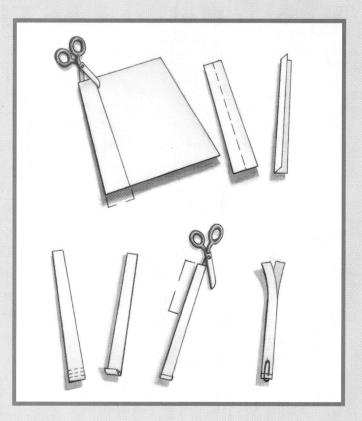

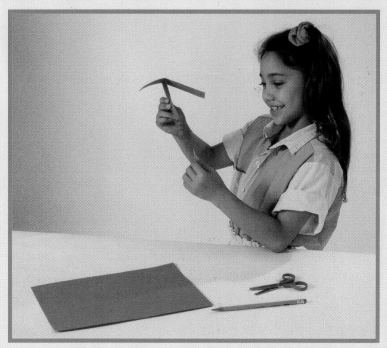

THINK AND WRITE

1. How do you think a rotor is different from a propeller?

2. **INTERPRETING DATA** When you interpret data, you decide what it means. Use the data you have gathered to explain why a helicopter flies differently than an airplane.

How a Helicopter Flies

The first helicopter flight took place in 1907. The helicopter tipped and shook. Four people on the ground had to steady it with ropes. The first helicopter that could really fly came in 1939. Since then, people have used helicopters in many ways.

Helicopters are amazing machines. They can fly like airplanes, and they can do a lot more. They can take off straight up into the air, and they can fly sideways and backward. They can fly very slowly and even stay still in one spot in the air.

What allows helicopters to do these things? Their wings make it possible. If you want to find a helicopter's wings, look at its top. The rotor blades on top of the helicopter are its wings.

Helicopter rotor blades are curved, like the wings and the propeller of an airplane. As they spin, the blades create lift. They pull the helicopter up.

Helicopter pilots can turn their machines in all directions by tilting the rotor blades. There is also a small rotor on a helicopter's tail. The small rotor helps the pilot steer. It also stops the helicopter from spinning around in a circle. Helicopters are harder to fly than airplanes. And most cannot fly as fast or as high as airplanes.

▲ The unique way helicopters fly makes it possible to use them to rescue people from the water.

Because of the way they fly, helicopters will always be useful. They are good for taking off, landing, and moving around in tight spaces. They can land on the small decks of ships. They can also land in the mountains and in other places without runways.

Because helicopters can fly slowly and stay in one spot, they are good for rescues in wilderness areas or at sea. Some helicopters, called sky cranes, carry very heavy loads. These giants help in building bridges and skyscrapers.

THINK ABOUT IT

Helicopters are used by some hospitals to move injured people. Why are helicopters especially useful for this job?

▲ Helicopters like this one are used to lift heavy loads.

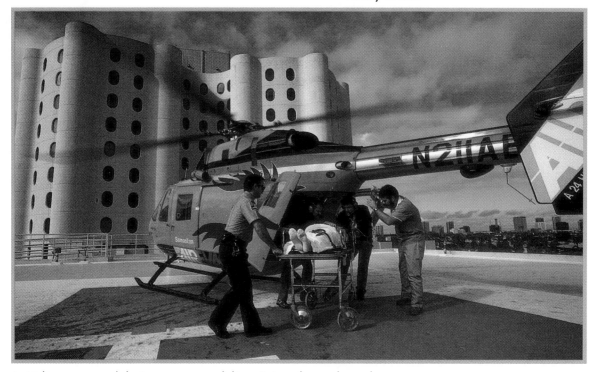

▲ Helicopters and their crews can deliver injured people to the hospital quickly.

"Helicopter" Fruits

The shape of a rotor can be found in nature. Perhaps this natural shape led people to invent the helicopter rotor.

Maple and ash trees have fruits that are shaped a lot like the rotor blades of a helicopter. Other trees have these winglike fruits, too.

If you can, watch a "helicopter" fruit as it falls from a tree. The fruit whirls like the rotors of a helicopter. Because of this, the fruit stays in the air longer. The wind can blow it farther. So new trees can grow farther from the parent tree.

▲ Each of these maple trees grew from a seed.

◀ In the spring, the fruits, which contain the seeds, are ready to fall to the ground.

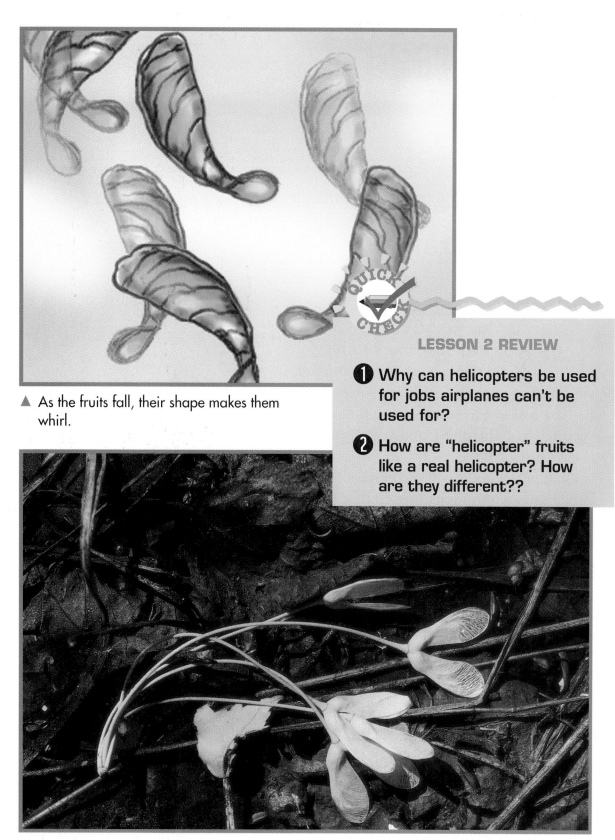

▲ As the fruits fall, their shape makes them whirl.

LESSON 2 REVIEW

❶ Why can helicopters be used for jobs airplanes can't be used for?

❷ How are "helicopter" fruits like a real helicopter? How are they different??

▲ The winged fruits can be carried far on the wind. Soon they will grow into new maple trees.

It takes more than machines to fly. It also takes many brave people. Now it's time to meet some of them.

Amelia Earhart

by **Peggy Mann**

from *A Challenge to Others*

▲ **Amelia Earhart**

LITERATURE The date was May 20, 1932, five years to the day after Charles A. Lindbergh had set out on the first solo flight across the Atlantic. Amelia Earhart was out to make her own world record, to be the first *woman* to fly across the Atlantic—alone.

Gradually she flew into darkness. Then, suddenly, something happened that had never occurred in all her twelve years of flying—the dials of the altimeter started to spin. She could no longer tell how high she was above the sea.

Rain hit against the windshield. Lightning whipped and cracked. The airplane was shaking in the fierce wind.

For an hour she fought the plane through the storm. If she could only rise high enough and fly above the clouds! She climbed for thirty minutes. Ice collected on the wings.

Then, one wing lurched up and snapped over. The plane spun, over and over, out of control toward the ocean.

With all her strength, Amelia drove the stick all the way forward. Somehow she brought the plane into control and nosed it up out of the dive.

Her heart thumping with terror, she looked down. She was a dangerous 100 feet above the water. Without the altimeter she could not risk flying too low over waves which she could not see. Yet she did not want to fly up again into the storm.

She flew on, hoping that the plane was strong enough to hold through the hours ahead. Finally, she flew into the first streaks of dawn. She turned on the reserve tanks—and saw she had a leaky gauge!

She *must* come down. Perhaps she was near the tip of Ireland. Ahead were low, hanging thunderclouds, and beneath them—mountains!

But where could she land? At last she saw a space of flat green. She landed her plane in an Irish pasture, near Londonderry. The flight had taken fourteen hours and fifty-six minutes, the longest minutes in Amelia's life.

▲ **Amelia Earhart with her plane in 1933**

Around the World

No man had ever tried it, not even Charles Lindbergh. Amelia wanted to fly around the world taking the longest route, at the equator.

June 1, 1937, was set as the takeoff date. The first stop was Puerto Rico. As her plane got closer to the island, a fishing pole with a note tied to it appeared over her left shoulder. The note, from navigator Fred Noonan, informed her that she was flying off course, too far south.

The next morning they took off from San Juan Airport for the 3,000-mile stretch along the coast of South America to Natal, the takeoff spot for their flight across the Atlantic to Africa. In all those 3,000 miles there were only four airfields. If they were forced to land anywhere in between, they would have to come down in dense jungle or in the ocean.

Last Flight

On June 30, Amelia made the long flight from Port Darwin, Australia, to Lae, New Guinea. She was tired. She had traveled over five continents, crossed the equator four times, and flown 22,000 miles in forty days. She was looking forward now to returning home.

Ahead of her lay the longest leg of the world flight, and the most dangerous. She would fly across 2,556 miles of Pacific Ocean to tiny Howland Island. If one of the navigation instruments were off even a little, Amelia and Fred would miss the island. From the air it was only a tiny speck of land surrounded by 7,000 miles of ocean.

At ten o'clock on the morning of July 2, 1937, Amelia Earhart's silver-winged airplane roared down the runway, a long strip cut out of the jungle. The plane headed up into the clouds.

The U.S. Coast Guard cutter *Itasca* lay anchored off Howland Island. The ship was to give Amelia regular radio bearings.

At 2:45 A.M., Amelia reported that the weather was "cloudy and overcast." Did that mean Fred Noonan was not able to use the stars for navigation?

At 7:42 in the morning Amelia's voice came in loud and clear. "We must be on you. But cannot see you. Gas is running low. Been unable to reach you by radio. We are flying at altitude 1,000 feet."

At 7:58, Amelia's voice came again. "We are circling, but cannot hear you!"

At 8:45, her voice came once more, broken and wild, giving her position.

That was Amelia Earhart's last message. She was never heard from again.

THINK ABOUT IT

Why is Amelia Earhart important to the history of flight?

Gale Carter
Ride with a Hurricane Hunter

When a hurricane comes, most people try to get away, but not Gale Carter. He likes hurricanes. He takes off and flies right into them.

Gale Carter is a *meteorologist*—a scientist who studies and predicts weather. The predictions of how hurricanes might move and how much damage they might do are important. Early warnings can move people from a storm's path and save lives.

Carter is also a lieutenant colonel in the U.S. Air Force Reserve's "Hurricane Hunter" unit. During hurricane season—June through November—unit members must always be ready to fly into a hurricane.

Why fly into a hurricane? "We need to know the exact position of the storm. We need to know the air pressure and the wind speed inside the storm," Carter says. The only way to learn these things is to fly inside.

Isn't flying into a hurricane dangerous? "Yes," says Carter. "But you get used to it. It's really like a roller-coaster ride. During Hurricane Andrew, I had to put my hand up to keep from hitting the ceiling," Carter says with a laugh.

During the flight, Carter is busy taking wind, pressure, and humidity readings in the storm. Another crew member drops instruments down through the storm's eye. The plane and the instruments transmit their data back to the National Hurricane Center in Coral Gables, Florida.

Gale Carter leaving on a flight ▶

▲ **Gale Carter checking the instruments on the plane**

There are 120 hurricane hunters. The men and women in this small group have a big job. Carter has flown into more than 100 hurricanes. "It's fun and exciting," says Carter. "Everyone else wants hurricanes to go away. But when a hurricane starts up, we can't wait to go out there."

LESSON 3 REVIEW

❶ Why are many fliers considered brave people? Do you think being brave makes a person a better pilot?

❷ Why do people fly into hurricanes?

DOUBLE CHECK

SECTION D REVIEW

1. Many early tests of flying machines were made without people or with animals. Why do you think this was so?

2. How has flying affected the lives of people? Do you think these changes are good or bad? Explain your answer.

Where No One Has Gone Before

First, fliers soared into the sky. Then, they looked to space.

The age of human spaceflight began on April 12, 1961. That's when Yuri Gagarin, a Russian cosmonaut, made the first orbit of Earth. His trip into space lasted just 1 hour 48 minutes. Since Gagarin's trip, astronauts and cosmonauts have circled Earth, walked in space, and have even walked on the moon.

You might not be flying a rocket or space shuttle anytime soon. But you can make models of them in this section. You can also explore how rockets work.

As you read, think about the progress in flight that people have made. Keep a record of your thoughts in your Science Log.

1 ROCKETS

How does a rocket take off into space?

Pop Goes the Rocket

Make a model rocket to discover the answers to some of your questions about rockets.

MATERIALS
- plastic squeeze bottle
- clay
- small plastic straw
- ruler
- large plastic straw
- scissors
- Science Log data sheet

DO THIS

1 Put a clay top on the bottle. Put the small straw into the opening of the bottle so that about 10 cm of the straw is sticking out of the top. Be careful not to plug the straw with the clay.

2 CAUTION: Scissors are sharp. Be careful not to cut yourself. Cut a piece about 10 cm long from the large straw. This is the straw rocket. Seal one end of the rocket with clay.

3 Slide the rocket over the small straw. The small straw is the launcher. Squeeze the plastic bottle quickly and hard. Watch what happens.

THINK AND WRITE

What happened to the straw rocket? Explain why you think this happened.

How Rockets Work

Real rockets don't have a bottle on the launch pad to push them away from Earth. A real rocket has the most powerful engine of any flying machine.

Rocket engines burn fuel in an area at the bottom of the rocket. The hot gases press on the inside walls of this area. The gases also rush out from under the rocket. They create a force that presses against the inside of the rocket and downward. That force, called *thrust*, lifts the rocket off the ground.

Rockets must create enough thrust to escape Earth's gravity. They must move at 40,200 kilometers per hour (24,974 miles per hour) to leave Earth.

To reach such high speeds, rockets must lift their own weight. A rocket and its fuel weigh a lot. Rockets are built in several parts, called *stages*, to make the lifting easier. Each stage has its own fuel supply. When each stage uses all its fuel, the stage drops off. This makes the rocket lighter, so it can then travel faster with less thrust.

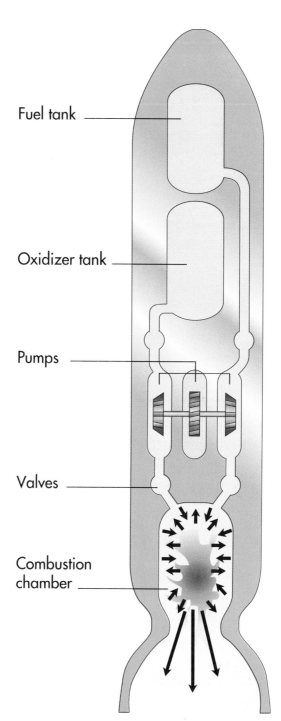

Fuel tank

Oxidizer tank

Pumps

Valves

Combustion chamber

The Chinese probably built the first rockets around the year A.D. 1000. Their "arrows of fire" were long bamboo tubes. The tubes had gunpowder inside. These early rockets were used as weapons.

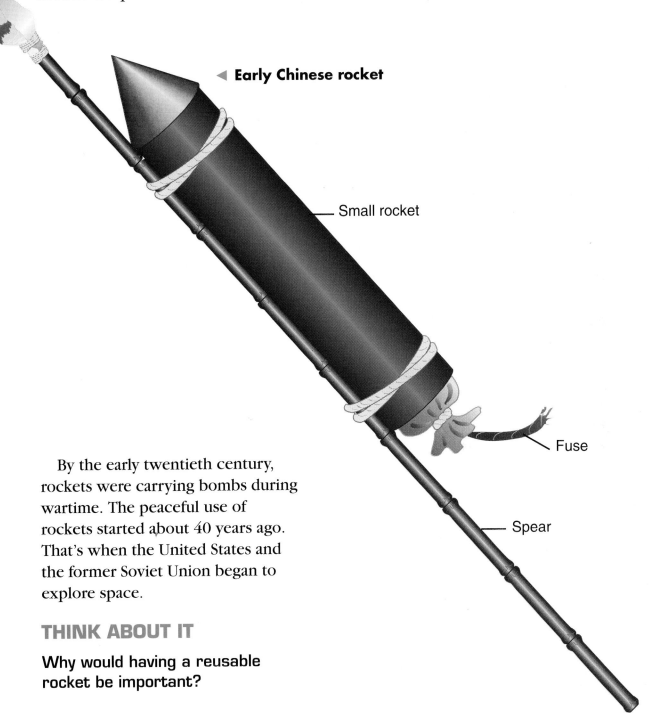

◀ **Early Chinese rocket**

— Small rocket

— Fuse

— Spear

By the early twentieth century, rockets were carrying bombs during wartime. The peaceful use of rockets started about 40 years ago. That's when the United States and the former Soviet Union began to explore space.

THINK ABOUT IT

Why would having a reusable rocket be important?

ACTIVITY

Make a Space-Shuttle Model

The space shuttle is the United States' reusable spacecraft. Build a model to learn more about the shuttle. Make the shuttle as shown in the picture.

MATERIALS

- 2 egg cartons
- scissors
- masking tape
- small paper cup
- 2–L plastic soda bottle
- newspaper
- glue for papier-mâché
- paint
- paintbrush
- Science Log data sheet

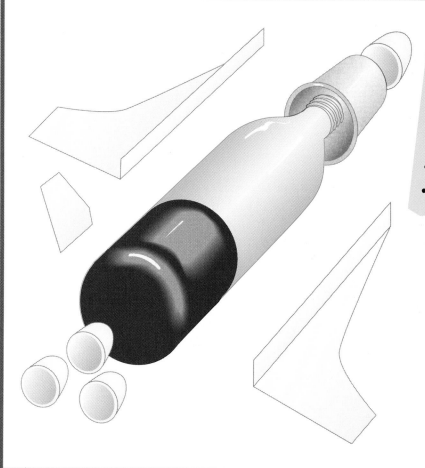

DO THIS

1 Cut out two wings from the top of an egg carton. Tape them as the picture shows.

2 Cut out an egg cup from the carton. Tape it to the bottom of the paper cup. Tape the paper cup over the neck of the bottle.

3 Cut out the tail from the top of the other egg carton. Tape it to the bottle.

4 Tear thin strips of newspaper. Glue them all over the bottle. Let the glue dry.

5 Cut out three more egg cups. Glue them to the bottom of the bottle. Let the glue dry.

6 Paint the model.

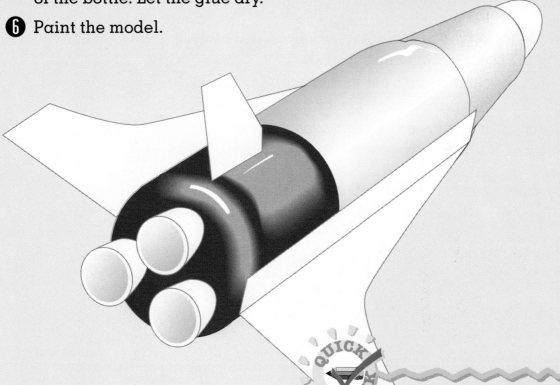

THINK AND WRITE

How is your model like the space shuttle? How is it different?

QUICK CHECK

LESSON 1 REVIEW

1 You blow up a balloon and hold it closed. Then you let it go. What happens? How is what happens to the balloon like the flight of a rocket?

2 How is the way a rocket travels different from the way an airplane does?

2 SATELLITES AND SPACE PROBES

Satellites and space probes are spacecraft with no people aboard. Satellites orbit Earth. Space probes travel on one-way journeys away from Earth. They are controlled by computer programs and by signals beamed from Earth.

These spacecraft can't get into space by themselves. Each is carried into space by a rocket or put into orbit by the space shuttle. In space the craft separates from the rocket and goes off on its own.

Space shuttle launching a satellite from the cargo bay ▼

Rockets, Probes, and Satellites

by **Isaac Asimov**
from ***Rockets, Probes, and Satellites***

We can see and hear things as they happen on the other side of our planet.

Since 1981, we have had space shuttles—spacecraft that can be used over and over again. Shuttles can carry satellites into space and place these satellites in orbit.

Rockets and Satellites at Work

Satellites do much more than circle the Earth. They do many kinds of work. Since 1958, for example, many communications satellites have been sent into orbit. They can receive radio waves from one place, make them stronger, and send them to a completely different place. Today, television programs and telephone calls can be sent easily from continent to continent.

Satellite in orbit around Earth ▶

▲ **This is what Hurricane Andrew looked like from a satellite.**

Forecasting the Weather

Weather satellites began to be sent up in 1960. While orbiting the Earth, they take photographs of Earth and send them down in the form of radio waves. When these radio waves are received on Earth, weather people

◄ **Weather satellite**

can create the satellite pictures we see on the news each night. For the first time in history, we can see the clouds covering all of the Earth and watch how they move. This makes it much easier to predict the weather. For example, we can see large circular cloud formations that make up hurricanes. Before 1960, we couldn't always tell when a hurricane might hit. Now people can board up their homes and leave before it comes. Countless lives have been saved in this way.

Satellite weather map of the United States ▼

Fact File: Rockets, Probes, and Satellites

Here is one look at the sky above. It gives you an idea of the incredible assortment of satellites that the nations of Earth have sent up. These satellites give us new ways of understanding our Earth and space, predicting the weather, communicating with one another, performing technological experiments, and even spying on one another.

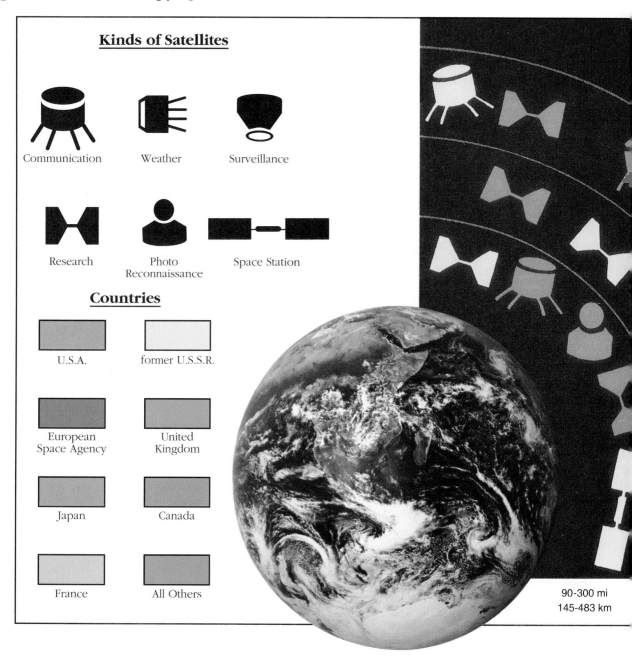

Kinds of Satellites

Communication

Weather

Surveillance

Research

Photo Reconnaissance

Space Station

Countries

U.S.A.

former U.S.S.R.

European Space Agency

United Kingdom

Japan

Canada

France

All Others

90-300 mi
145-483 km

Many space probes have been launched from Earth. They have explored Mercury, Venus, Mars, and the Moon. But the journeys of the two Voyager spacecraft have been even grander.

THINK ABOUT IT

Tell about one way a spacecraft has affected your life.

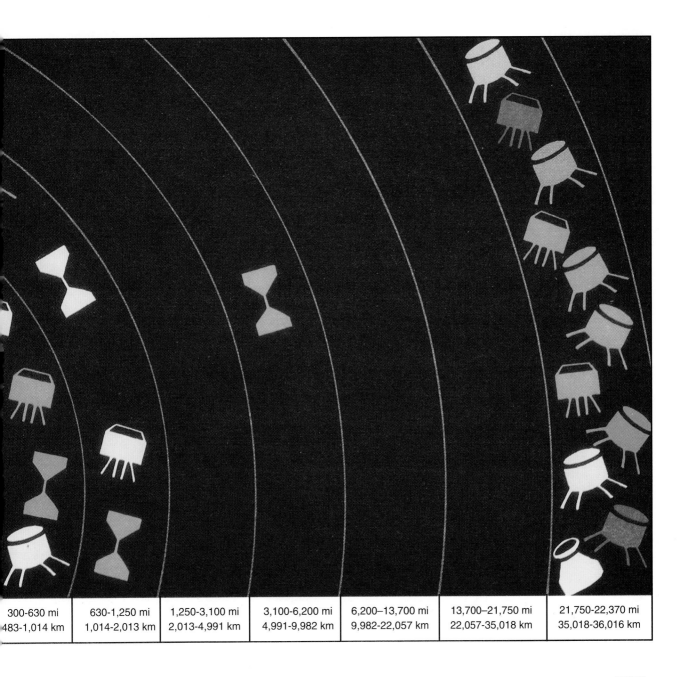

300-630 mi	630-1,250 mi	1,250-3,100 mi	3,100-6,200 mi	6,200–13,700 mi	13,700–21,750 mi	21,750-22,370 mi
483-1,014 km	1,014-2,013 km	2,013-4,991 km	4,991-9,982 km	9,982-22,057 km	22,057-35,018 km	35,018-36,016 km

The Voyagers' Long Trips

Two Voyager probes have been sent into space. These probes have provided much information about our solar system.

Voyager 1 left Earth on September 5, 1977. It flew by both Jupiter and Saturn. Two weeks earlier, *Voyager 2* had left on a still longer trip.

Voyager 2 traveled for many years through the solar system. It beamed back close-up views of Jupiter, Saturn, Uranus, and Neptune.

Voyager 2 sent its data back to Earth, where computers received it. The computers turned the data into the beautiful color photos you see in this section. Because of *Voyager 2*, we now know a lot more about the rings of Saturn and the moons of Jupiter. *Voyager 2* has also let us see the icy surfaces of Uranus and Neptune.

◀ *Voyager 2* began its journey through the solar system on August 20, 1977.

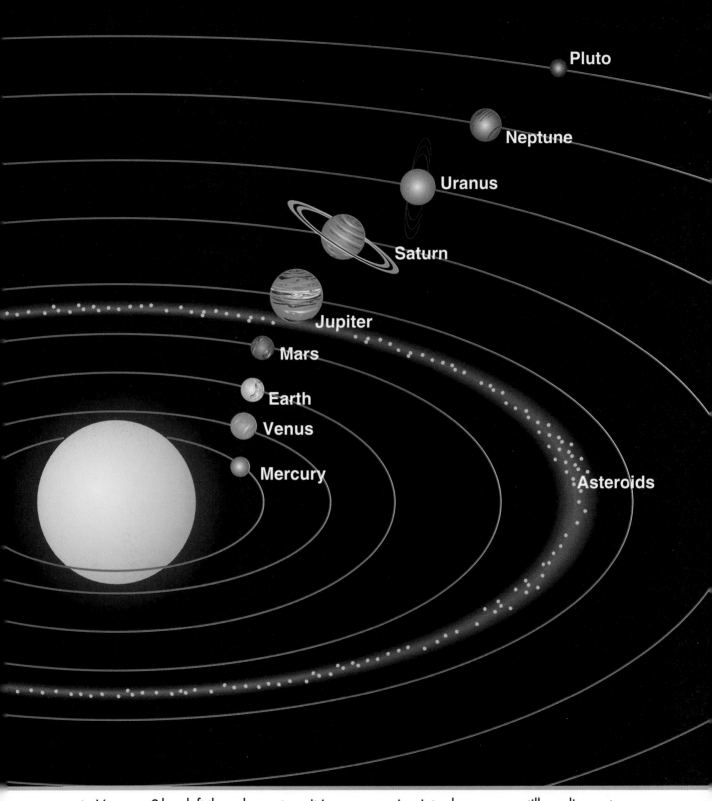

Pluto

Neptune

Uranus

Saturn

Jupiter

Mars

Earth

Venus

Mercury

Asteroids

▲ *Voyager 2* has left the solar system. It is now zooming into deep space, still sending out signals. *Voyager 1* is also still working. The Voyagers will keep sending their signals back to Earth for years. If we can still hear them, who knows what they might tell us?

◀ *Voyager 2* flew past Jupiter in 1979. It took this picture of Jupiter and its tiny moon.

Voyager 2 reached Saturn in 1981. Here is Saturn as seen through *Voyager 2's* cameras. ▶

◀ In 1986 *Voyager 2* passed by Uranus at 67,000 kilometers per hour (41,623 miles per hour). It's shown in the background here. Look carefully for its thin rings.

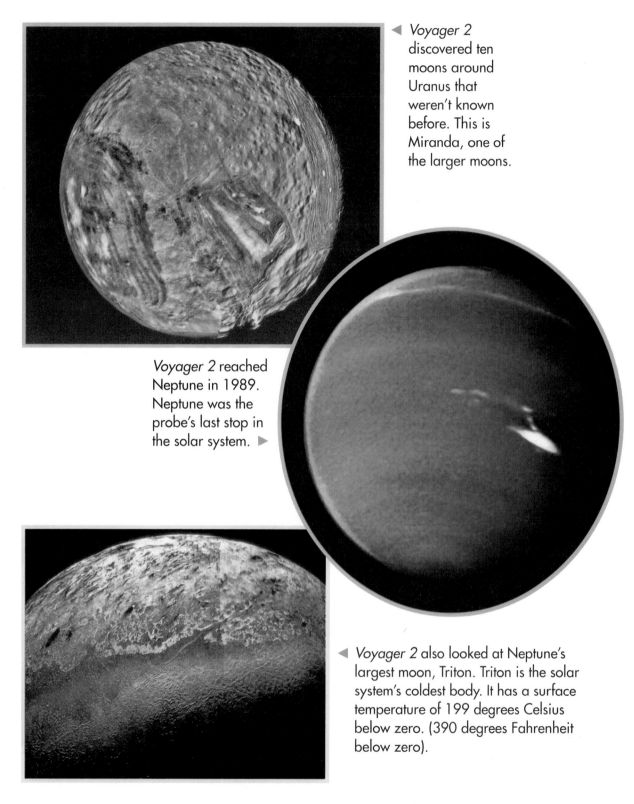

◄ *Voyager 2* discovered ten moons around Uranus that weren't known before. This is Miranda, one of the larger moons.

Voyager 2 reached Neptune in 1989. Neptune was the probe's last stop in the solar system. ▶

◄ *Voyager 2* also looked at Neptune's largest moon, Triton. Triton is the solar system's coldest body. It has a surface temperature of 199 degrees Celsius below zero. (390 degrees Fahrenheit below zero).

THINK ABOUT IT

Why do you think the outer planets are so cold?

The Inner Planets

The Voyager probes flew past the outer planets of our solar system—Jupiter, Saturn, Uranus, and Neptune. Other probes have taken pictures of the inner planets—Mercury, Venus, and Mars.

◄ Mercury is the planet closest to the sun. It is rocky, like all the inner planets. It has no atmosphere and no moons. Mercury's rocky surface was photographed by *Mariner 10*, a space probe launched in 1973. ▼

Venus is the planet between Mercury and Earth. It has a thick atmosphere. It is so thick that probes can't take pictures of the surface. ► Instead, probes like *Magellan* use radar to map the surface. ▼

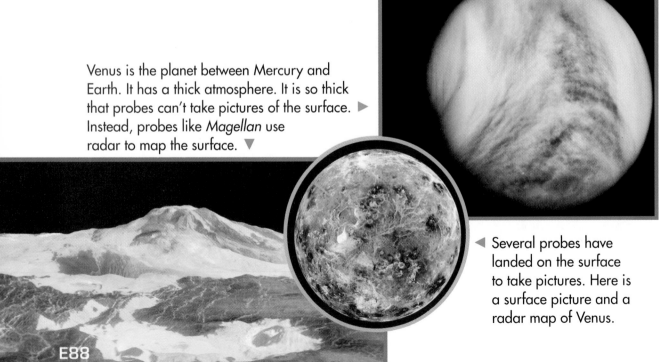

◄ Several probes have landed on the surface to take pictures. Here is a surface picture and a radar map of Venus.

◀ Mars is the fourth planet from the sun. Its surface is covered with red dust that makes it look red when viewed from Earth. Mars has been photographed by several probes, including *Viking I* and *Viking II*. These probes landed on the surface and took close-up pictures. ▼

LESSON 2 REVIEW

1 How have rockets made satellites and space probes possible?

2 Explain how satellites and space probes are alike and different.

DOUBLE CHECK

SECTION E REVIEW

1. Describe two ways people use satellites and two things people have learned from space probes.

2. Helicopters and rockets can both lift off straight into the air. How are the ways they lift off different?

E89

I REFLECT

It's time to think about the ideas you have discovered during your investigations. Think, too, about your many accomplishments.

SUMMARIZE

Answer the following in your **Science Log.**

1. What **I Wonder** questions have you answered in your investigations? What new questions have you asked?

2. What have you discovered about air and flying? How have your ideas changed?

3. Did any of your discoveries surprise you? Explain.

Things I Found Out About Flight

I found out that wind is moving air. Some things can fly through the air. People have always wanted to find out how to fly.

Kites and blimps are things that people have flown. I made a paper airplane. I found out how different forces help my plane fly.

CONNECT IDEAS

1. The dark side of the moon gets no sunlight and is very cold. The temperature remains nearly the same all the time. If the moon had air, could there be wind on the dark side? Explain your answer.

2. Name some things that flight makes possible.

3. Think about the shape of an airplane. How is this shape like the shape of many animals that fly, such as birds and bats?

4. Airplanes have to travel very fast to stay in the air. Why is this so?

SCIENCE PORTFOLIO

❶ Complete your Science Experiences Record.

❷ Select a few samples of your best work from each section to include in your Science Portfolio.

❸ On A Guide to My Science Portfolio, tell why you chose each sample.

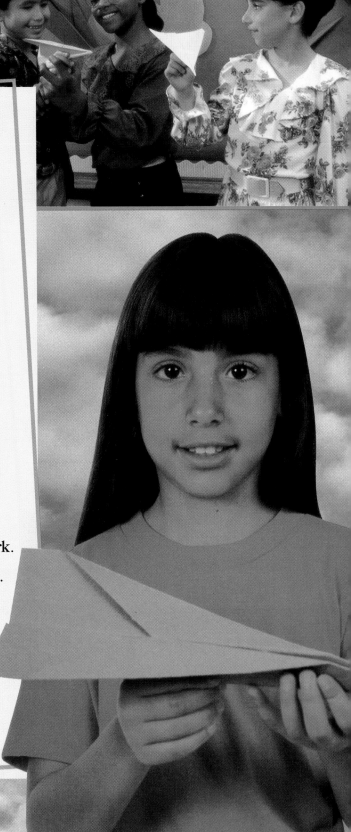

I SHARE

Scientists share their discoveries and ideas and learn from one another. How can you share what you've learned?

Decide

▶ what you want to say.

▶ what the best way is to get your message across.

Share

▶ what you did and why.

▶ what worked and what didn't work.

▶ what conclusions you have drawn.

▶ what else you'd like to find out.

Find Out

▶ what classmates liked about what you shared—and why.

▶ what questions they have.

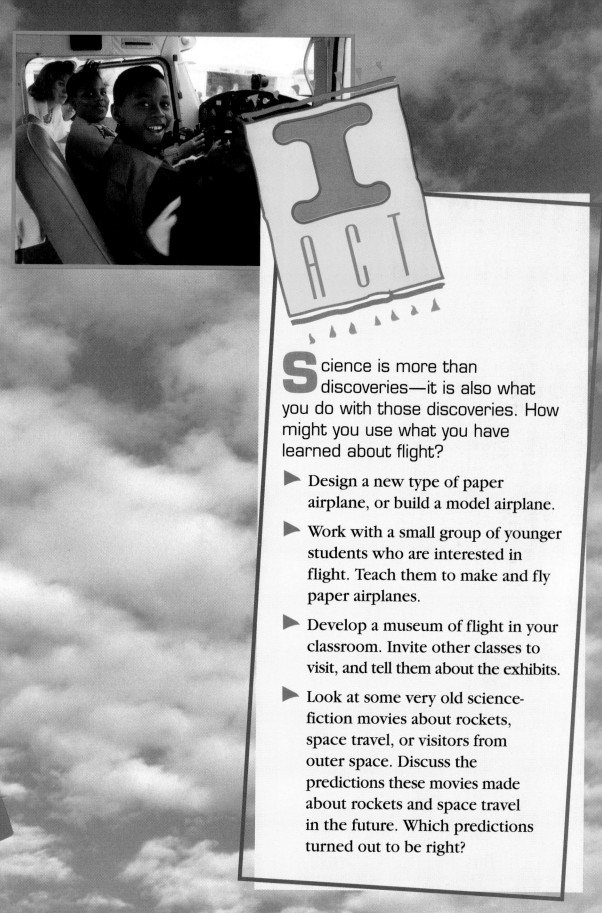

I ACT

Science is more than discoveries—it is also what you do with those discoveries. How might you use what you have learned about flight?

► Design a new type of paper airplane, or build a model airplane.

► Work with a small group of younger students who are interested in flight. Teach them to make and fly paper airplanes.

► Develop a museum of flight in your classroom. Invite other classes to visit, and tell them about the exhibits.

► Look at some very old science-fiction movies about rockets, space travel, or visitors from outer space. Discuss the predictions these movies made about rockets and space travel in the future. Which predictions turned out to be right?

THE LANGUAGE OF SCIENCE

The language of science helps people communicate clearly when they talk about flight. Here are some vocabulary words you can use when you talk about flight with friends, family, and others.

air pressure—the force that air exerts on objects **(E16)**

drag—the force of air that pushes against the forward movement of an airplane **(E51)**

force—a push or pull that acts on objects **(E51)**

helicopter—an aircraft that uses a spinning rotor on its top to lift straight up and fly **(E62)**

▲ **Helicopter**

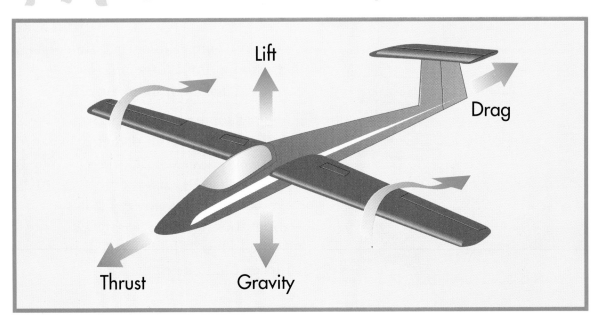

Lift

Drag

Thrust

Gravity

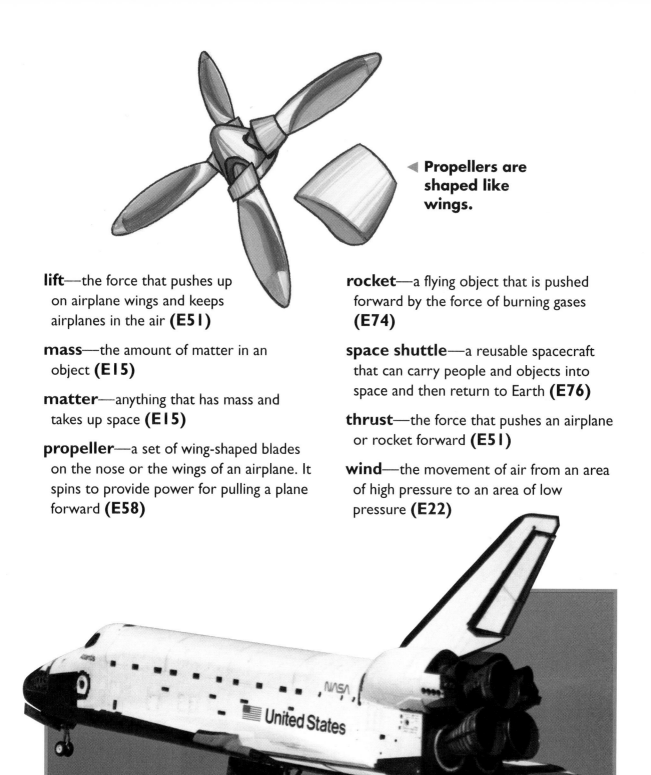

◀ **Propellers are shaped like wings.**

lift—the force that pushes up on airplane wings and keeps airplanes in the air **(E51)**

mass—the amount of matter in an object **(E15)**

matter—anything that has mass and takes up space **(E15)**

propeller—a set of wing-shaped blades on the nose or the wings of an airplane. It spins to provide power for pulling a plane forward **(E58)**

rocket—a flying object that is pushed forward by the force of burning gases **(E74)**

space shuttle—a reusable spacecraft that can carry people and objects into space and then return to Earth **(E76)**

thrust—the force that pushes an airplane or rocket forward **(E51)**

wind—the movement of air from an area of high pressure to an area of low pressure **(E22)**

▲ **Space shuttle landing**

REFERENCE HANDBOOK

Safety in the Classroom

Doing activities in science can be fun, but you need to be sure you do them safely. It is up to you, your teacher, and your classmates to make your classroom a safe place for science activities.

Think about what causes most accidents in everyday life—being careless, not paying attention, and showing off. The same kinds of behavior cause accidents in the science classroom.

Here are some ways to make your classroom a safe place.

WATCH YOUR EYES.

Wear safety goggles anytime you are directed to do so. If you should ever get any substance in your eyes, tell your teacher right away.

THINK AHEAD.

Study the steps of the activity so you know what to expect. If you have any questions about the steps, ask your teacher to explain. Be sure you understand any safety symbols that are shown in the activity.

BE NEAT.

Keep your work area clean. If you have long hair, pull it back so it doesn't get in the way. If you have long sleeves, roll them or push them up to keep them away from your experiment.

YUCK!

Never eat or drink anything during a science activity unless you are told to do so by your teacher.

OOPS!

If you should have an accident that causes a spill or breaks something, or if you get cut, tell your teacher right away.

DON'T GET SHOCKED.

Sometimes you need to use electric appliances, such as lamps, in an activity. You always need to be careful around electricity. Be sure that electric cords are in a safe place where you can't trip over them. Don't ever pull a plug out of an outlet by pulling on the cord.

KEEP IT CLEAN.

Always clean up when you have finished your activity. Put everything away and wipe your work area. Last of all, wash your hands.

Safety Symbols

In some activities, you will see a symbol that stands for what you need to do to stay safe. Do what the symbol stands for.

 This is a general symbol that tells you to be careful. Reading the steps of the activity will tell you exactly what you need to do to be safe.

 You will need to protect your eyes if you see this symbol. Put on safety goggles and leave them on for the entire activity.

 This symbol tells you that you will be using something sharp in the activity. Be careful not to cut or poke yourself or others.

 This symbol tells you something hot will be used in the activity. Be careful not to get burned or to cause someone else to get burned.

 This symbol tells you to put on an apron to protect your clothing.

 Don't touch! This symbol tells you that you will need to touch something that is hot. Use a thermal mitt to protect your hand.

 This symbol tells you that you will be using electric equipment. Use proper safety procedures.

Using a Hand Lens

A hand lens magnifies objects, or makes them look larger than they are.

▲ **This object is not in focus.**

Sometimes objects are too small for you to see easily without some help. You might want to see details that you cannot see with your eyes alone. When this happens, you can use a hand lens.

To use a hand lens, first place the object you want to look at on a flat surface, such as a table. Next, hold the hand lens over the object. At first, the object may appear blurry, like the object in **A**. Move the hand lens toward or away from the object until the object comes into sharp focus, as shown in **B**.

▲ **This object is focused clearly.**

Making a Water-Drop Lens

There may be times when you want to use a hand lens but there isn't one around. If that happens, you can make a water-drop lens to help you in the same way a hand lens does. A water-drop lens is best used to make flat objects, such as pieces of paper and leaves, seem larger.

MATERIALS
- sheet of acetate
- 2 rectangular rubber erasers
- water
- dropper

DO THIS

1 Place the object to be magnified on a table between two identical erasers.

2 Place a sheet of acetate on top of the erasers so that the sheet of acetate is about 1 cm above the object.

3 Use the dropper to place one drop of water on the surface of the sheet over the object. Don't make the drop too large or it will make things look bent.

A water-drop lens can magnify objects. ▶

Caring For and Using a Microscope

A microscope, like a hand lens, magnifies objects. However, a microscope can increase the detail you see by increasing the number of times an object is magnified.

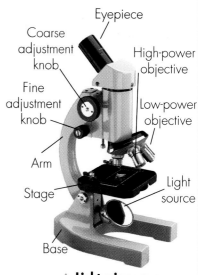

▲ **Light microscope**

CARING FOR A MICROSCOPE

• Always use two hands when you carry a microscope.
• Never touch any of the lenses of the microscope with your fingers.

USING A MICROSCOPE

1 Raise the eyepiece as far as you can using the coarse-adjustment knob. Place the slide you wish to view on the stage.

2 Always start by using the lowest power. The lowest-power lens is usually the shortest. Start with the lens in the lowest position it can go without touching the slide.

3 Look through the eyepiece and begin adjusting the eyepiece upward with the coarse-adjustment knob. When the slide is close to being in focus, use the fine-adjustment knob.

4 When you want to use the higher-power lens, first focus the slide under low power. Then, watching carefully to make sure that the lens will not hit the slide, turn the higher-power lens into place. Use only the fine-adjustment knob when looking through the higher-power lens.

Some of you may use a Brock microscope. This is a sturdy microscope that has only one lens.

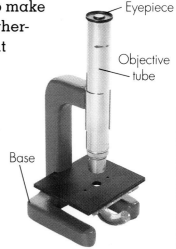

1 Place the object to be viewed on the stage. Move the long tube, containing the lens, close to the stage.

2 Put your eye on the eyepiece, and begin raising the tube until the object comes into focus.

▲ **Brock microscope**

Using a Dropper

Use a dropper when you need to add small amounts of a liquid to another material.

A dropper has two main parts. One is a large empty part called a *bulb*. You hold the bulb and squeeze it to use the dropper. The other part of a dropper is long and narrow and is called a *tube*.

DO THIS

1. Use a clean dropper for each liquid you measure.

2. With the dropper out of the liquid, squeeze the bulb and keep it squeezed. Then dip the end of the tube into the liquid.

3. Release the pressure on the bulb. As you do so, you will see the liquid enter the tube.

4. Take the dropper from the liquid, and move it to the place you want to put the liquid. If you are putting the liquid into another liquid, do not let the dropper touch the surface of the second liquid.

5. Gently squeeze the bulb until one drop comes out of the tube. Repeat slowly until you have measured out the right number of drops.

▲ Using a dropper correctly

▲ Using a dropper incorrectly

Measuring Liquids

Use a beaker, a measuring cup, or a graduated cylinder to measure liquids accurately.

Containers for measuring liquids are made of clear or translucent materials so that you can see the liquid inside them. On the outside of each of these measuring tools, you will see lines and numbers that make up a scale. On most of the containers used by scientists, the scale is in milliliters (mL).

DO THIS

1 Pour the liquid you want to measure into one of the measuring containers. Make sure your measuring container is on a flat, stable surface, with the measuring scale facing you.

2 Look at the liquid through the container. Move so that your eyes are even with the surface of the liquid in the container.

3 To read the volume of the liquid, find the scale line that is even with the top of the liquid. In narrow containers, the surface of the liquid may look curved. Take your reading at the lowest point of the curve.

4 Sometimes the surface of the liquid may not be exactly even with a line. In that case, you will need to estimate the volume of the liquid. Decide which line the liquid is closer to, and use that number.

▲ There are 32 mL of liquid in this graduated cylinder.

▲ There are 27 mL of liquid in this beaker.

Using a Thermometer

Determine temperature readings of the air and most liquids by using a thermometer with a standard scale.

Most thermometers are thin tubes of glass that are filled with a red or silver liquid. As the temperature goes up, the liquid in the tube rises. As the temperature goes down, the liquid sinks. The tube is marked with lines and numbers that provide a temperature scale in degrees. Scientists use the Celsius scale to measure temperature. A temperature reading of 27 degrees Celsius is written 27°C.

DO THIS

1 Place the thermometer in the liquid whose temperature you want to record, but don't rest the bulb of the thermometer on the bottom or side of the container. If you are measuring the temperature of the air, make sure that the thermometer is not in direct sunlight or in line with a direct light source.

2 Move so that your eyes are e the liquid in the thermomete

3 If you are measuring a material that is not being heated or cooled, wait about two minutes for the reading to become stable. Find the scale line that meet the top of the liquid in the thermometer, and read the temperature.

4 If the material you are measuring is being heated o cooled, you will not be able t wait before taking your measurements. Measure as quickly as you can.

The temperature of this liquid is 27°C. ▶

Making a Thermometer

If you don't have a thermometer, you can make a simple one easily. The simple thermometer won't give you an exact temperature reading, but you can use it to tell if the temperature is going up or going down.

DO THIS

❶ Add colored water to the jar until it is nearly full.

❷ Place the straw in the jar. Finish filling the jar with water, but leave about 1 cm of space at the top.

❸ Lift the straw until 10 cm of it stick up out of the jar. Use the clay to seal the mouth of the jar.

❹ Use the dropper to add colored water to the straw until the straw is at least half full.

❺ On the straw, mark the level of the water. "S" stands for *start*.

❻ To get an idea of how your thermometer works, place the jar in a bowl of ice. Wait several minutes, and then mark the new water level on the straw. This new water level should be marked C for *cold*.

❼ Take the jar out of the bowl of ice, and let it return to room temperature. Next, place the jar in a bowl of warm water. Wait several minutes, and then mark the new water level on the straw. This level can be labeled W for *warm*.

MATERIALS

- small, narrow-mouthed jar
- colored water
- clear plastic straw
- ruler
- clay
- dropper
- pen, pencil, or marker
- bowl of ice
- bowl of warm water

—W

—S

—C

▶ You can use a thermometer like this to decide if the temperature of a liquid or the air is going up or down.

Using a Balance

Use a balance to measure an object's mass. Mass is the amount of matter an object has.

Most balances look like the one shown. They have two pans. In one pan, you place the object you want to measure. In the other pan, you place standard masses. Standard masses are objects that have a known mass. Grams are the units used to measure mass for most scientific activities.

DO THIS

❶ First, make certain the empty pans are balanced. They are in balance if the pointer is at the middle mark on the base. If the pointer is not at this mark, move the slider to the right or left. Your teacher will help if you cannot balance the pans.

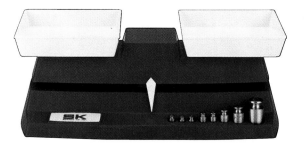

◄ **These pans are balanced and ready to be used to find the mass of an object.**

❷ Place the object you wish to measure in one pan. The pointer will move toward the pan without the object in it.

❸ Add the standard masses to the other pan. As you add masses, you should see the pointer begin to move. When the pointer is at the middle mark again, the pans are balanced.

❹ Add the numbers on the masses you used. The total is the mass of the object you measured.

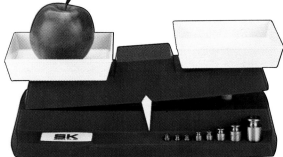

These pans are unbalanced. ▶

Making a Balance

If you do not have a balance, you can make one. A balance requires only a few simple materials. You can use nonstandard masses such as paper clips or nickels. This type of balance is best for measuring small masses.

DO THIS

MATERIALS
- 1 sturdy plastic or wooden ruler
- string
- transparent tape
- 2 paper cups
- 2 large paper clips

1 If the ruler has holes in it, tie the string through the center hole. If it does not have holes, tie the string around the middle of the ruler.

2 Tape the other end of the string to a table. Allow the ruler to hang down from the side of the table. Adjust the ruler so that it is level.

3 Unbend the end of each paper clip slightly. Push these ends through the paper cups as shown. Attach each cup to the ruler by using the paper clips.

4 Adjust the cups until the ruler is level again.

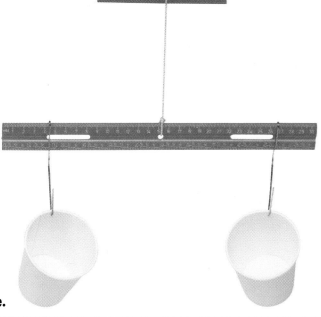

▶ This balance is ready for use.

Using a Spring Scale

A spring scale is a tool you use to measure the force of gravity on objects. You find the weight of the objects and use newtons as the unit of measurement for the force of gravity. You also use the spring scale and newtons to measure other forces.

A spring scale has two main parts. One part is a spring with a hook on the end. The hook is used to connect an object to the spring scale. The other part is a scale with numbers that tell you how many newtons of force are acting on the object.

DO THIS

With an Object at Rest

> With the object resting on the table, hook the spring scale to it. Do not stretch the spring at this point.
>
> Lift the scale and object with a smooth motion. Do not jerk them upward.
>
> Wait until any motion in the spring comes to a stop. Then read the number of newtons from the scale.

With an Object in Motion

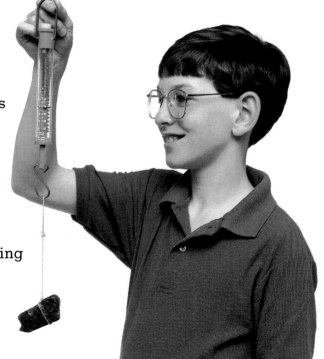

> With the object resting on the table, hook the spring scale to it. Do not stretch the spring.
>
> Pull the object smoothly across the table. Do not jerk the object. If you pull with a jerky motion, the spring scale will wiggle too much for you to get a good reading.
>
> As you are pulling, read the number of newtons you are using to pull the object.

Making a Spring Scale

If you do not have a spring scale, you can make one by following the directions below.

DO THIS

MATERIALS
- heavy cardboard (10cm x 30cm)
- large rubber band
- stapler
- marker
- large paper clip
- paper strip (about 1 cm x 3 cm)
- 100-g masses (about 1 N each)

1 Staple one end of the rubber band (the part with the sharp curve) to the middle of one end of the cardboard so that the rubber band hangs down the length of the cardboard. Color the loose end of the rubber band with a marker to make it easy to see.

2 Bend the paper clip so that it is slightly open and forms a hook. Hang the paper clip by its unopened end from the rubber band.

3 Put the narrow paper strip across the rubber band, and staple the strip to the cardboard. The rubber band and hook must be able to move easily.

4 While holding the cardboard upright, hang one 100-g mass from the hook. Allow the mass to come to rest, and mark the position of the bottom of the rubber band on the cardboard. Label this position on the cardboard 1 N. Add another 100-g mass for a total of 200 g.

5 Continue to add masses and mark the cardboard. Each 100-g mass adds a force of about 1 N.

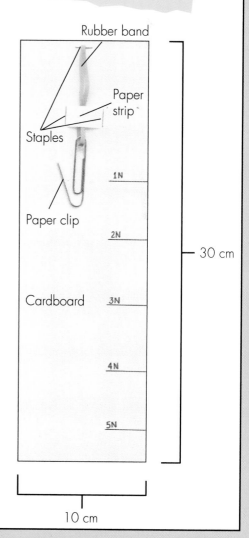

Working Like a Scientist
What Do Rabbits Like to Eat?

Have you ever wanted to know about something but you didn't know how to find out about it? Working like a scientist can help. Read the story below to find out how Alita, Juan, and Jasmine learned to work like scientists.

Alita, Juan, and Jasmine were friends. Each of them owned a rabbit. "I'd like to give my rabbit a treat," Alita told Juan and Jasmine. "I want the treat to be something that my rabbit likes. It should also be good for the rabbit."

"What do you think the best treat would be?" Juan asked.

"That's a good question," Jasmine said. "How can we find out the answer?"

Asking a good question is the first step in working like a scientist. A good question helps you find out what the problem is. A good question starts you on the way to finding an answer. Often a good question will have many answers.

DO THIS

| Ask a question. |
| Form a hypothesis. |
| Design a test. Do the test. |
| Record what happened. |
| Draw a conclusion. |

R14

After you ask a good question, you need to choose one possible answer and then find out if your answer is right. This possible answer to your question is called a *hypothesis*. You *form a hypothesis* when you choose an answer to a question. Sometimes you must do research before you can choose an answer. Find out how Alita, Juan, and Jasmine formed their hypothesis.

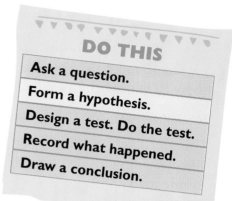

DO THIS

| Ask a question. |
| Form a hypothesis. |
| Design a test. Do the test. |
| Record what happened. |
| Draw a conclusion. |

The next day, Alita, Juan, and Jasmine met at Alita's house. Juan and Jasmine had brought their rabbits in their carrying cages.

"We need to find out what the best treat for a rabbit would be," Juan said.

Alita said, "My grandpa told me that rabbits like all kinds of vegetables. Maybe vegetables would be the best treat."

"I gave my rabbit some celery once and she didn't eat it at all. I wonder if my rabbit is different," Juan replied.

Jasmine said, "Why don't we say that we think rabbits like carrots, celery, and broccoli? Then we could test our rabbits to see if we're right."

"Yes," Alita said. "We can offer each rabbit carrots, celery, and broccoli and see what each one likes best."

"That sounds like a good idea," Juan said.

When Jasmine said to *do a test*, she was talking about doing an experiment. An experiment must be carefully designed and planned. You must decide how to do your test and how to record the results.

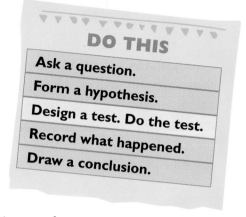

DO THIS

Ask a question.

Form a hypothesis.

Design a test. Do the test.

Record what happened.

Draw a conclusion.

Alita said, "We can put the three kinds of vegetables in each cage. We can watch our rabbits and see which vegetables they eat."

Jasmine said, "But we should do the test when we know our rabbits aren't very hungry. If they were, they might eat anything. I know that when I'm very hungry, I eat anything."

"That's true," Juan said. "And we shouldn't put one vegetable closer to the rabbit than the other vegetables. The rabbit might eat the first vegetable it saw. It might not eat the vegetable it liked best."

Alita said, "That sounds good. Let me write that down."

Jasmine said, "I've been thinking about our test. How are we going to know what the answer is? We should be able to say why we're giving our rabbits a certain kind of treat."

Juan said, "That's a good question. We have to find a way to record what our rabbits do."

Alita smiled. She showed Juan and Jasmine a chart.

"I made up this chart. It has a place for each rabbit and each kind of vegetable. We can see which vegetable each rabbit eats first."

DO THIS

| Ask a question. |
| Form a hypothesis. |
| Design a test. Do the test. |
| Record what happened. |
| Draw a conclusion. |

A Rabbit's Favorite Treat

	Broccoli			Carrots			Celery		
	1st	2nd	3rd	1st	2nd	3rd	1st	2nd	3rd
Jasmine's Rabbit									
Juan's Rabbit									
Alita's Rabbit									

What Alita showed Juan and Jasmine was a way to record what they saw the rabbits do. This is called *recording data.* It is an important part of science because it helps you explain why you think one answer may be right and another may be wrong.

Alita, Juan, and Jasmine put broccoli, carrots, and celery into the three rabbit cages. Alita's rabbit smelled the broccoli and then hopped to the carrots.

The rabbit ate some of the carrots, but it did not eat the celery. Jasmine's rabbit ate the carrots and a little bit of the celery. Juan's rabbit ate only the carrots.

Alita filled in the chart, and the three friends looked at it. Jasmine said, "It looks as if all three rabbits like carrots. My rabbit likes celery. None of the rabbits like broccoli."

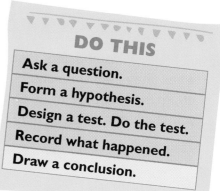

DO THIS

| Ask a question. |
| Form a hypothesis. |
| Design a test. Do the test. |
| Record what happened. |
| Draw a conclusion. |

A Rabbit's Favorite Treat	Broccoli			Carrots			Celery		
	1st	2nd	3rd	1st	2nd	3rd	1st	2nd	3rd
Jasmine's Rabbit				X				X	
Juan's Rabbit				X					
Alita's Rabbit				X					

What Jasmine did is *draw a conclusion*. She looked at the results of the test and was able to say what she thought the test showed. Just doing a test is not enough. You must be able to say what the test showed you.

"We haven't tried all vegetables," Juan said.

"No," Alita said. "And we didn't measure how much of the carrots and celery Jasmine's rabbit ate."

"We can do more tests," Jasmine said.

"All right," Alita said. "That would be fun!"

Juan said, "But for now, we know that our rabbits like carrots. So we can give them carrots for treats."

INDEX

Note: *Page numbers in italics indicate illustrations.*

animals without
backbones, A48
defined, A23
fish, A45
reptiles, A46
swamp, *A36*
Hail, *B35*
Halfpenny, James, A67–A71
Handrails, *C49*
Hang glider, *E2, E47*
Health
and air pollution, B66–B67
kitten's, A82–A83
Heart, and pollution,
B66–B67
Heavy-equipment operator,
C66–C67
Helicopters, *E60–E65, E62,
E63, E94*
activity, E60–E61
defined, E62, E94
uses of, E60, E62–E63
Helicopter seeds, *E64–E65*
Helium, E35
Heron, *D42*
Hibernation, *A65–A66*
Hibernators, A68
Hindenburg, E35
Hirschi, Ron, A9
Hockey puck, *C34*
Holstein cows, A72
Hooks (on quills), *A58*
Hookworm, *A49*
Horned frog, *A25*
Horns, as defense, A56
Horses, *A12, A74*
Hot-air balloon, *E26, E30, E32,
E33*
activity, E30–E31
how it flies, E33
parts of, E32
See also Balloon;
Weather balloon
*How the Guinea Fowl Got
Her Spots* (Knutson),
A8
Humidity
activities, B26, B29
defined, B27, B79
water vapor and, B26–B30

Hummingbird, egg of, *A79*
Hurricane, *E80, E81*
Hydrogen, E35
Hypothesizing, R15

Ice, in Antarctica, B25
Identifying variables, D63,
E10
Impala, *A54*
Imperial thorny oyster, *A39*
Inclined plane, *C6, C59–C61*
defined, C59, C78
See also Ramp
Inertia, *C44–C51, C45, C49,
C50*
activity, C46–C47
defined, C44, C79
protection from, C49–C51
Inferring, A10, A63, A87, C10,
C37
Insects
activity, A86–A87
camouflage of, *A24–A25*
in ponds, D15–16, D46–D47
Interpreting data, B10, B29,
E10, E25
It's an Armadillo! (Lavies),
A33–A35

Jack Miner Bird Sanctuary
(Kingsville, Ontario,
Canada), *A62, A63, A64*
Jackson Elementary School
(Everett, WA), D66–D71
James Bay (Canada),
A62, A63
Japanese garden pond,
D26–D27
Japanese wind poems, E18
Jellyfish, *A48*
Jennings, Terry, C9

Jumpers, frogs as,
D31–D32
Jupiter, E84, *E85, E86*

Kangaroo rat, *A14*
Kellet's whelk, *A39*
Kingdoms, *A40–A41*
Kites, *E38, E44–E49, E44–E45,
E46, E47, E48, E49*
activity, E48–E49
uses of, E45
Kitten, *A80–A83*
health of, A82–A83
movements of, A82–A83
play of, A82–A83
skills of, A82–A83
teeth of, A82
Kitty Hawk (NC), E58
Knutson, Barbara, A8

Kobayashi, Joy, D72–D73
Lake
activity, D50
artificial, *D6*
Lake Huron, *C69*
Lake Michigan, *C69*
Language of science
adaptation, A20, *A94,* D31,
D78
air pollution, B59, B78
air pressure, B45, B78, E16,
E94
axis, B19, B78
barometer, B46, *B78*
camouflage, A23, *A94*
cirrus clouds, B33, *B78*
classify, A38, A94
compound machine, C64,
C78
condensation, B27, *B79*
consumers, D40, D78
cumulus clouds, B33, *B79*

ACKNOWLEDGMENTS

For permission to reprint copyrighted material, grateful acknowledgment is made to the following sources:

Mel Boring: From "The Bridge That Couldn't Be Built" in *Cricket* Magazine, June 1991. Text © by Mel Boring.

Carolrhoda Books, Inc., Minneapolis, MN: Cover illustration from *How the Guinea Fowl Got Her Spots* by Barbara Knutson. Copyright © 1990 by Barbara Knutson.

Children's Better Health Institute, Indianapolis, IN: From "Magic Jumpson" (originally titled "The Froggie") in *Jack and Jill* Magazine, March 1991. Text copyright © 1988 by Children's Better Health Institute, Benjamin Franklin Literary & Medical Society, Inc.

Coward, McCann & Geoghegan: Abridged from "Amelia Earhart" by Peggy Mann in *Amelia Earhart, First Lady of Flight.* Text copyright © 1970 by Peggy Mann.

Current Health 1® Magazine: "Can Rain Be Dangerous?" from *Current Health 1®* Magazine, November 1991. Text copyright © 1991 by Weekly Reader Corporation. Published by Weekly Reader Corporation.

Dial Books for Young Readers, a division of Penguin Books USA Inc.: Cover illustration from *Bridges* by Ken Robbins. Copyright © 1991 by Ken Robbins.

Doubleday, a division of Bantam Doubleday Dell Publishing Group, Inc.: Cover illustration from *Why Can't I Fly?* by Ken Brown. Copyright © 1990 by Ken Brown.

Dutton Children's Books, a division of Penguin Books USA Inc.: From *It's an Armadillo!* by Bianca Lavies. Copyright © 1989 by Bianca Lavies.

Farrar, Straus & Giroux, Inc.: "Ribbons of Wind" from *Balloons and Other Poems* by Deborah Chandra. Text copyright © 1988, 1990 by Deborah Chandra.

Frank Fretz: Illustration by Frank Fretz from "Only the Tough Survive" by James Halfpenny in *Ranger Rick* Magazine, December 1993.

Harcourt Brace & Company: Cover illustration from *A River Ran Wild* by Lynne Cherry. Copyright © 1992 by Lynne Cherry.

The Hokuseido Press, Tokyo, Japan: Untitled haiku (Retitled: "Japanese Poem") by Buson from *Haiku,* Vols. 1-4, translated by R. H. Blyth.

Holiday House, Inc.: Cover illustration from *Weather Words and What They Mean* by Gail Gibbons. Copyright © 1990 by Gail Gibbons.

Richard Lewis: Untitled poem (Retitled: "African Bushman Poem") from *Out of the Earth I Sing,* edited by Richard Lewis. Text copyright © 1968 by Richard Lewis.

Little, Brown and Company: From *Four Corners of the Sky: Poems, Chants and Oratory* (Retitled: "Native American Kiowa Verse"), selected by Theodore Clymer. Text copyright © 1975 by Theodore Clymer.

Little, Brown and Company, in Association with Arcade Publishing, Inc.: Cover illustration by Ted Rand from *Water's Way* by Lisa Westberg Peters. Illustration copyright © 1991 by Ted Rand.

Lothrop, Lee & Shepard Books, a division of William Morrow & Company, Inc.: Cover illustration by Catherine Stock from *Galimoto* by Karen Lynn Williams. Illustration copyright © 1990 by Catherine Stock.

National Wildlife Federation: "Amazing Jumping Machine" by Carolyn Duckworth from *Ranger Rick* Magazine, March 1991. Text copyright 1991 by the National Wildlife Federation. "Only the Tough Survive" by James Halfpenny from *Ranger Rick* Magazine, December 1993. Text copyright 1993 by the National Wildlife Federation. Drawings by Jack Shepherd from "Magic Jumpson" in *Ranger Rick* Magazine, March 1991. Copyright 1991 by the National Wildlife Federation.

North-South Books Inc., New York: Cover illustration from *The Air Around Us* by Eleonore Schmid. Copyright © 1992 by Nord-Sud Verlag AG, Gossau Zürich, Switzerland.

Marian Reiner: Untitled haiku (Retitled: "Japanese Poem") by Asayasu from *More Cricket Songs,* translated by Harry Behn. Text copyright © 1971 by Harry Behn.

Sierra Club Books for Children: From *Come Back, Salmon* by Molly Cone. Text copyright © 1992 by Molly Cone.

Simon & Schuster Books for Young Readers, New York: Cover illustration from *Frog Odyssey* by Juliet and Charles Snape. © 1991 by Juliet and Charles Snape.

Gareth Stevens, Inc., Milwaukee, WI: From *Rockets, Probes, and Satellites* by Isaac Asimov. Text © 1988 by Nightfall, Inc.

Walker and Company: Cover illustration by Valerie A. Kells from *One Earth, a Multitude of Creatures* by Peter and Connie Roop. Illustration copyright © 1992 by Valerie A. Kells.

PHOTO CREDITS

Key: (t)top, (b)bottom, (l)left, (r)right, (c)center, (bg)background.

Front Cover, All Other Photographs: (tl), Robert Maier/Animals Animals; (tr), NASA/International Stock Photo; (c), Jean-Francois Causse/Tony Stone Images; (cr), Kristian Hilsen/Tony Stone Images; (bl), Benn Mitchell/The Image Bank; (br), E.R. Degginger/Color-Pic.
Back Cover, Harcourt Brace & Company Photographs: (t), Greg Leary; (bl), Earl Kogler.
Back Cover, All Other Photographs: (br), Kaz Mori/The Image Bank.
To The Student, Harcourt Brace & Company Photographs: vi(tr), vi(c), Weronica Ankarorn; vi(b), Maria Paraskevas; viii, Earl Kogler; xv(b), Jerry White.
To The Student, All Other Photographs: iv(tl), Neena Wilmot/Stock/Art Images; iv(tr), Jane Burton/Bruce Coleman, Inc.; iv(bl), Dwight R. Kuhn; iv(br), Dave B. Fleetham/Tom Stack & Assoc.; v(t), Dave Bartruff; v(b), Photri; vi(tl), W. Hille/Leo de Wys, Inc.; vii(l), Stephen Dalton/Photo Researchers; vii(r), John Gerlach/Tom Stack & Assoc.; x, David Young-Wolff/PhotoEdit; xi(t), T. Rosenthal/SuperStock; xi(b), Gabe Palmer/The Stock Market; xii, Myrleen Ferguson Cate/PhotoEdit; xiii, Tony Freeman/PhotoEdit; xiv(l), Jeff Greenberg/Photo Researchers; xiv(r), Russell D. Curtis/Photo Researchers; xv(t), Bob Daemmrich; xvi(l), Myrleen Ferguson Cate/PhotoEdit; xvi(r), Bob Daemmrich/Stock, Boston.
Unit A, Harcourt Brace & Company Photographs: A4-A5, A6(t), A7, Dick Krueger; A8, A9, Weronica Ankarorn; A10-A11, Dick Krueger; A16(r), A17(tr), A17(b), A19, A20(b), A22, A27, A37, A38, A43(l), A44, Earl Kogler; A63, Eric Camden; A76, A86, Earl Kogler; A92-A93(bg), David Lavine; A92(t), A93, Earl Kogler.
Unit A, All Other Photographs: Unit Page Divider, Erwin & Peggy Bauer; A1, A2-A3, Alan & Sandy Carey; A3, Hugh P. Smith, Jr.; A6(b), Alan Briere/SuperStock; A12(bg), Index Stock; A12(t), David R. Frazier; A12(b), William Johnson/Stock, Boston; A13(t), Henry Ausloos/Animals Animals; A13(b), Antoinette

Jongen/SuperStock; A14(t), John Cancalosi/Stock, Boston; A14(b), M. Bruce/SuperStock; A15(t), Stephen G. Maka/Lightwave; A15(b), H. Lanks/SuperStock; A16(l), G. Corbett/SuperStock; A17(tl), Stephen J. Krasemann/NHPA; A20(t), M. Burgess/SuperStock; A21, A. Mercieca/SuperStock; A23(t), Dwight R. Kuhn; A23(b), James T. Jones/David R. Frazier Photolibrary; A24(t), SuperStock; A24(b), Stephen G. Maka/Lightwave; A25(t), Gary Bell/The Wildlife Collection; A25(cl), Larry A. Brazil; A25(cr), Stephen J. Krasemann/Valan Photos; A25(b), David Cavagnaro/Peter Arnold, Inc.; A28, The Granger Collection; A30(tl), A. Kaiser/SuperStock; A30(tr), Stephen Dalton/NHPA; A30(b), Aaron Haupt/David R. Frazier Photolibrary; A31, A32(t), SuperStock; A32(c), John Giustina/The Wildlife Collection; A32(b), Sven-Olaf Lindblad/Photo Researchers; A33(t), A33(b), A34(t), A34(c), A34(b), A35(l), A35(r), Bianca Lavies; A36(bg), Rod Planck/Tony Stone Images; A36(t), Scot Stewart; A36(b), Stephen G. Maka/Lightwave; A39(tl), Bill Tronca/Tom Stack & Assoc.; A39(tc), A39(tr), T. Wolf Bolz/TexStockPhotoInc.; A39(bl), David M. Dennis/Tom Stack & Assoc.; A39(bc), Claudio Ferer/Devaney Stock Photos; A39(br) Gerald & Buff Corsi/Tom Stack & Assoc.; A40, Leonard Lee Rue III/Animals Animals; A41, Tetsu Yamazaki; A42, Bob Daemmrich/The Image Works; A43(r), Don Enger/Animals Animals; A45(l), Ron & Valerie Taylor/Bruce Coleman, Inc.; A45(r), A46(t), Zig Leszczynski/Animals Animals; A46(cl), E.R. Degginger/Color-Pic; A46(cr), Renee Lynn/Photo Researchers; A46(b), Holton Collection/SuperStock; A47(tl), Alan G. Nelson/Animals Animals; A47(tr), E.R. Degginger/Animals Animals; A47(c), Fred Whitehead/Animals Animals; A47(b), Dominique Braud/Tom Stack & Assoc.; A48(t), Brian Parker/Tom Stack & Assoc.; A48(b), Oxford Scientific Films/Animals Animals; A49(tl), Dwight R. Kuhn; A49(tc), Lester V. Bergman & Assoc.; A49(tr), Rod Planck/Tom Stack & Assoc.; A49(cl), Biophoto Associates/Photo Researchers; A49(cr), John Shaw/Tom Stack & Assoc.; A49(b), Dave B. Fleetham/Tom Stack & Assoc.; A52(bg), Tim Fitzharris/Masterfile; A52(t) H. Morton/SuperStock; A52(b), John Cancalosi/Valan Photos; A53, D. Robert Franz/The Wildlife Collection; A54(tl), Stephen G. Maka/Lightwave; A54(tr), Hank Andrews/Visuals Unlimited; A54(b), Mike Bacon/Tom Stack & Assoc.; A55(t), Stephen G. Maka/Lightwave; A55(b), SuperStock; A56(t), Stephen G. Maka/Lightwave; A56(c), Gerald & Buff Corsi/Tom Stack & Assoc.; A56(b), Fred Bruemmer/Valan Photos; A57(t), Scot Stewart; A57(b), Western History Department/Denver Public Library; A58(tl), A58(tr), Daniel W. Gotshall; A58(bl) SuperStock; A58(br), Dwight R. Kuhn; A59(t), SuperStock; A59(b), John Cancalosi/Valan Photos; A61(t), M. Bruce/SuperStock; A61(b), SuperStock; A62-A63(bg), Index Stock; A64(t) A64(b) Master's Studio; A65, Jane Burton/Bruce Coleman, Inc.; A66, Mark Sherman/Bruce Coleman, Inc.; A67, Michael S. Quinton; A68(t), Erwin & Peggy Bauer; A68(bl), Frank Fretz; A68(br), Erwin & Peggy Bauer; A69, Stephen J. Krasemann/DRK; A70, Leonard Lee Rue III; A71, Erwin & Peggy Bauer; A72(bg), Gregory Dimijian/Photo Researchers; A72(t), John Colwell/Grant Heilman Photography; A72(b), H. Mark Weidman; A73, David R. Frazier; A74(t), Allen Russell/ProFiles West; A74(c), Doug Perrine/Innerspace Visions; A74(b), John Cancalosi/Tom Stack & Assoc.; A75(t), John Fowler/Valan Photos; A75(cl), Dwight R. Kuhn; A75(cr), Stephen G. Maka/Lightwave; A75(b), Martin Harvey/The Wildlife Collection; A77, Wolfgang Kaehler; A78(t), Dr. Paul V. Loiselle; A78(b), John T. Pennington/Ivy Images; A79, Martin Harvey/The Wildlife Collection; A80, A81(t), A81(b), A82(t), A82(cl), A82(cr), A82(b), A83(t), Dwight R. Kuhn; A83(bl), A83(br), Renee Stockdale/Animals Animals; A84(tl), Dwight R. Kuhn; A84(tr), Tom & Pat Leeson/DRK; A84(bl), Mella

Panzella/Animals Animals; A84(br), Neena Wilmot/Stock/Art Images; A85(tl), Gary Braasch; A85(tr), Brian Parker/Tom Stack & Assoc.; A85(cl), A85(c), SuperStock; A85(cr), Gary Braasch; A85(b), A88(t), A88(cl), A88(cr), A88(b), A89(l), A89(r), Dwight R. Kuhn; A90-A91, Index Stock; A91(l), SuperStock; A91(r), A. Briere/SuperStock; A92(b), Allen Russell/ProFiles West; A94(t), Sven-Olaf Lindblad/Photo Researchers; A94(c), Anthony J. Bond/Valan Photos; A94(b), Stephen J. Krasemann/Valan Photos; A95(l), Wolfgang Bayer/Bruce Coleman, Inc.; A95(r), A. Mercieca/SuperStock.

Unit B, Harcourt Brace & Company Photographs: B4-B5, B6(t), B7(t), B7(b), Dick Krueger; B8, B9, Weronica Ankarorn; B10-B11, Maria Paraskevas; B14, B15, B16, B17, B20, Earl Kogler; B23(cb), Rodney Jones; B28(bc), B29(t), B29(b), B30, B36, B37, Earl Kogler; B40(bg), David Phillips; B41, B42, Earl Kogler; B43, Richard Nowitz; B44, B46(t), B46(b), B47, B53, Earl Kogler; B55(t), B55(b), B56(l), B56(r), B57, Jerry Heasley; B61, B63, B68, Richard T. Nowitz; B76(t), B76(b), Earl Kogler; B77(b), Richard T. Nowitz; 79(t), Earl Kogler.

Unit B, All Other Photographs: Unit Page Divider, A. Farquhar/Valan Photos; B1, Amy Drutman; B2-3, Gordon Wiltsie/Peter Arnold, Inc.; B3, Alan & Sandy Carey; B6(c), R. Dahlquist/SuperStock; B6(b), George Cargill/Lightwave; B12(bg), Jay Maisel; B12, Scott Barrow; B18(l), B18(r), B19(l), B19(r), E.R. Degginger/Bruce Coleman, Inc.; B22(t), SuperStock; B22(ct), David R. Frazier; B22(cb), Scott Barrow; B22(b), Hans & Judy Beste/Earth Scenes; B23(t), Scott Barrow; B23(ct), Harry M. Walker; B23(b), Loren McIntyre; B24(tl), Will & Deni McIntyre/AllStock; B24(tr), Tony Freeman/PhotoEdit; B24(cl), J.C. Carton/Bruce Coleman, Inc.; B24(cr), Richard T. Nowitz; B24(b), Fotoconcept; B25(t), John Eastcott, Yva Momatiuk/Valan Photos; B25(b), Sovfoto; B27, David Falconer/David R. Frazier Photolibrary; B28(bg), Dwight R. Kuhn; B28(t), Steve Solum/Bruce Coleman, Inc.; B28(bl), David R. Frazier; B28(br), Dave Bartruff; B32-B33, Gary Black/Masterfile; B32, Peter Griffith/Masterfile; B33, Mark Tomalty/Masterfile; B34, Peter Miller/Photo Researchers; B35(t), Alan Hicks/AllStock; B35(c), Wouterloot-Gregoire/Valan Photos; B35(b), Joyce Photographics/Valan Photos; B36-B37(bg), Dick Thomas/Visuals Unlimited; B40(t), Phil Degginger/Color-Pic; B40(b), Tony Freeman/PhotoEdit; B48, The Granger Collection; B50(bg), John Running/Stock, Boston; B50, The Granger Collection; B51(t) David R. Frazier; B51(b), Photri; B52, Runk, Schoenberger/Grant Heilman Photography; B54(l), A. Farquhar/Valan Photos; B54(r), SuperStock; B58(bg), David Woodfall/Tony Stone Images; B58(t), E.R. Degginger/Color-Pic; B58(b), Jose L. Pelaez/The Stock Market; B59, R. Llewellyn/SuperStock; B60(t), E.R. Degginger/Color-Pic; B60(c), Tony Freeman/PhotoEdit; B60(b), Anna Zuckerman/PhotoEdit; B62-B63(bg), E.R. Degginger/Color-Pic; B64, B65, B66, David R. Frazier; B67, Tony Freeman/PhotoEdit; B69, Ruth Dixon; B70, North Wind; B71, Phil Degginger/Color-Pic; B72(t), Bill Weedmark; B72(b), Dave Bartruff; B73, Grapes Michaud/Photo Researchers; B74-B75, J.R. Page/Valan Photos; B75(t), Valerie Wilkinson/Valan Photos; B75(b), SuperStock; B76-B77(bg), Greg Vaughn/Tom Stack & Assoc.; B77(t), Aaron Haupt/David R. Frazier Photolibrary; B78(t), Runk, Schoenberger/Grant Heilman Photography; B78(b), Mark Tomalty/Masterfile; B79(c) Gary Black/Masterfile; B79(b), John Heseltine/Photo Researchers; B80(l), Peter Griffith/Masterfile; B80(r), A. Upitis/SuperStock.

Unit C, Harcourt Brace & Company Photographs: C4-C5, C6(c), C6(b), C7(t), David Phillips; C7(c), Earl Kogler; C7(b), David Phillips; C8, C9, Weronica Ankarorn; C10-C11, C13, C14(b), C15(t), C15(bl), C15(br), C16, C17, C19(tl), C19(tr), C19(b), Earl Kogler; C20-C21(bg), Jerry White; C20, C21(t), C21(bl), C21(br),

C22(tr), C22(br), C23(tl), C23(c), C23(b), C24, C25, C28(l), C28(c), C28(r), C29(t), C29(b), Earl Kogler; C32(t), Gerald Ratto; C35, Earl Kogler; C36, C37, C39, C40, C43(t), C43(c), C43(b), C45(t), Dick Krueger; C45(b), Rob Downey; C46-C47(bg), Dick Krueger; C46, C47, Weronica Ankarorn; C48, Dick Krueger; C52(b), C53, Maria Paraskevas; C54(t), Bruce Wilson; C54(cl), Weronica Ankarorn; C54(cr), Earl Kogler; C54(b), Weronica Ankarorn; C55, Earl Kogler; C56(t), C56(b), C57(t), Maria Paraskevas; C58, Earl Kogler; C59(t), C59(b), Maria Paraskevas; C60, C61, C63(t), C63(b), C64, Earl Kogler; C66(t), C66(b), C67, Robert Landau; C73, C75(t), Earl Kogler; C75(b), David Phillips; C76(t), Earl Kogler; C76(b), David Phillips; C77, Jerry White; C78(l), Earl Kogler; C79(tl), Bruce Wilson; C79(tr), Earl Kogler; C79(bl), David Phillips; C79(br), Earl Kogler.

Unit C, All Other Photographs: Unit Page Divider, Bud Nielsen/Lightwave; C1, Richard T. Nowitz/Valan Photos; C2-C3, David R. Frazier; C3, Rapho/Photo Researchers; C6(t), SuperStock; C12(bg), Harold Sund/The Image Bank; C12(t), James Blank/Zephyr Pictures; C12(b), W. Hille/Leo de Wys, Inc.; C14(t), Terry Wild Studio; C14(c), Ewing Galloway; C22(l), T. Matsumoto/Sygma; C23(tr), E.R. Degginger/Earth Scenes; C24-C25(bg), NASA; C26, The Bettmann Archive; C27, Lewis Portnoy/Spectra-Action; C30, Christopher Liu/ChinaStock; C31(t), Milt & Joan Mann/Cameramann; C31(b), Harry M. Walker; C32(b), Robert Frerck/Odyssey Productions; C33, Yves Tessier/Tessima; C34(bg), Roy Ooms/Masterfile; C34(t), John Terence Turner/FPG; C34(b), Alissa Crandall; C38-C39(bg), SuperStock; C41, Paul Souders/AllStock; C42(t), David R. Frazier; C42(c), C42(b), Alan & Sandy Carey; C44, NASA/Photri; C49, Dave Bartruff; C50-C51(bg), William Warren/West Light; C50(all), C51(all), Insurance Institute for Highway Safety; C52(bg), Index Stock; C52(t), Bud Nielsen/Lightwave; C57(b), Neena M. Wilmot/Stock/Art Images; C62(t), Ruth Dixon; C62(c), Dave Bartruff; C62(b), Aldo Mastrocola/Lightwave; C68, Steinman, Boynton, Gronquist & Birdsall; C70-C71, Frederic Stein/FPG; C72-C73(bg), Ken Graham; C74-C75(bg), SuperStock; C76-C77(bg), Andrew Sacks/Tony Stone Images; C78(r), Lewis Portony/Spectra-Action.

Unit D, Harcourt Brace & Company Photographs: D4-D5, Earl Kogler; D6(t), Dick Krueger; D8, D9, Weronica Ankarorn; D10-D11, D22, D23(b), Earl Kogler; D24, Earl Kogler; D25, D26-D27, Britt Runion; D37(t), D37(b), D60(t), D62(t), D62(b) D63, D64, D65, Earl Kogler; D72, D73, Robert Landau; D76, D77(t), Richard T. Nowitz; D77(b), Earl Kogler.

Unit D, All Other Photographs: Unit Page Divider, Mark J. Thomas/Dembinsky Photo Assoc; D1, D2-D3, Larry Lefever/Grant Heilman Photography; D3, Adam Jones/Dembinsky Photo Assoc.; D6(b), William McKinney/FPG; D7, Neena M. Wilmot/Stock/Art Images; D12(bg), Greg Nikas/Viesti Assoc.; D12(t), David R. Frazier; D12(b), Ruth Dixon; D13, Rod Planck/Tom Stack & Assoc.; D14(t), M.P.L. Fogden/Bruce Coleman, Inc.; D14(b), E.R. Degginger/Bruce Coleman, Inc.; D15(t), S. Maimone/SuperStock; D15(b), John Gerlach/Tom Stack & Assoc.; D16-D17(bg), Gabe Palmer/The Stock Market; D16, Gary Meszaros/Dembinsky Photo Assoc.; D17, John Shaw/Bruce Coleman, Inc.; D18(t), Mark J. Thomas/Dembinsky Photo Assoc.; D18(b), J.H. Robinson/Photo Researchers; D19, Gay Bumgarner/Photo Network; D23(t), Patti Murray/Earth Scenes; D28-D29, Betsy Blass/Photo Researchers; D29(tl), Karl H. Switak/Photo Researchers; D29(tr), E.R. Degginger/Color-Pic; D30(bg), Stephen G. Maka/Lightwave; D30(t), Stephen Dalton/Photo Researchers; D30(b), Stephen J. Krasemann/Valan Photos; D31, Stephen Dalton/Photo Researchers; D32(t), Zig Leszczynski/Animals Animals; D32(c), J.H. Robinson/Animals Animals; D32(b), Zig Leszczynski/Animals Animals; D33(t), Kim

Taylor/Bruce Coleman, Inc.; D33(b), Gregory Dimijian/Photo Researchers; D38(t), D38(b), D39(t), D39(c), D39(b), Dwight R. Kuhn; D44(bg), SuperStock; D44(t), P. Van Rhijn/SuperStock; D44(b), Bob & Clara Calhoun/Bruce Coleman, Inc.; D46, D47 Dwight R. Kuhn; D48(t), Mildred McPhee/Valan Photos; D48(cl), Bill Beatty/Wild & Natural; D48(cr), E.R. Degginger/Color-Pic; D48(cb), Glen D. Chambers; D48(bl), J. Faircloth/Transparencies; D48(br), Oxford Scientific Films/Anmo Animals; D49(t), J.A. Wilkinson/Valan Photos; D49(cl), Bill Beatty/Wild & Natural; D49(cr), Steve Maslowski/Valan Photos; D49(cb), Thomas Kitchin/Tom Stack & Assoc.; D49(bl), Bill Beatty/Wild & Natural; D49(br), John Shaw/Bruce Coleman, Inc.; D54, Phillip Norton/Valan Photos; D56-D57, Manley/SuperStock; D56, John Eastcott, Yva Momatiuk/Stock, Boston; D58(bg), R. Dahlquist/SuperStock; D58(t), M. Roessler/SuperStock; D58(b), D59, SuperStock; D60(b), Mark E. Gibson; D61(t), Dwight R. Kuhn; D61(b), A. Hennek/SuperStock; D66, D67(t), D67(b), D68, D69, D70(tl), D70(tr), D70(b), Sidnee Wheelwright; D71(t), Chris Huss/The Wildlife Collection; D71(c), D71(b), Sidnee Wheelwright; D74-D75(bg), SuperStock; D75, Nancy Sefton/Photo Researchers; D76-D77(bg), Andy Caulfield/The Image Bank; D78, James H. Carmichael, Jr./The Image Bank.

Unit E, Harcourt Brace & Company Photographs: E4-E5, Weronica Ankarorn; E6(t), Earl Kogler; E6(b), Dick Krueger; E8, E9, Weronica Ankarorn; E10-E11, E13, E14(t), E14(b), E15, Earl Kogler; E16, Weronica Ankarorn; E17, E20, E23, E24, E27, E29, E30, E38(t), E41(t), E41(b), E50, E57, E61, Earl Kogler; E91(r), Dick Krueger; E92(t), Earl Kogler; E92(b), Maria Paraskevas; E93, Dick Krueger.

Unit E, All Other Photographs: Unit Page Divider, Frank P. Rossotto/The Stock Market; E1, E2-E3, Neena M. Wilmot/Stock/Art Images; E2, Archiv/Photo Researchers; E3, Frank P. Rossotto/The Stock Market; E7, Milt & Joan Mann/Cameramann; E12(bg), Craig Aurness/West Light; E12(t), Allen S. Stone/Devaney Stock Photos; E12(b), Kennon Cooke/Valan Photos; E21, Wide World Photos; E26(bg), M. Stephenson/West Light; E26(t), K. Sklute/SuperStock; E26(b) North Wind; E30-E31(bg), Alese & Mort Pechter/The Stock Market; E33, Ron Watts/Black Star; E35, Linc Cornell/Light Sources; E38(bg), J.A. Kraulis/Masterfile; E38(b), Norman Owen Tomalin/Bruce Coleman, Inc.; E40(t), Russ Kinne/Comstock; E40(b), Spencer Swanger/Tom Stack & Assoc.; E47, William Carter/Photo Researchers; E54(bg), Paul Chesley/Tony Stone Images; E54(t), Steve Kaufman/Ken Graham Agency; E54(b), UPI/Bettmann; E55(tl), Percy Jones/Archive Photos; E55(tr), Photri; E55(c), Charles Palek/Tom Stack & Assoc.; E55(bl), Photri; E55(br), Frank P. Rossotto/Tom Stack & Assoc.; E60(l), Richard P. Smith/Tom Stack & Assoc.; E60(r), Ken Gouvin/Comstock; E62, Gerald & Buff Corsi/Tom Stack & Assoc.; E63(t), Gary Benson/Comstock; E63(b), John McDermott/Tony Stone Images; E64(t), Neena M. Wilmot/Stock/Art Images; E64(b), John Shaw/Tom Stack & Assoc.; E65, Bruce Matheson/PHOTO/NATS; E66, Archive Photos; E67, UPI/Bettmann Newsphotos; E68, The Bettmann Archive; E70, E71, U.S. Air Force; E72(bg), NASA; E72(t), NASA/Photri; E72(b), E78, NASA; E79, J. Novak/SuperStock; E80(t), Hank Brandli and Rob Downey; E80(b), European Space Agency/Photo Researchers; E81, David R. Frazier; E82, NASA/Photri; E84, E86(t), E86(c), NASA; E86(b), E87(t), Frank P. Rossotto/Tom Stack & Assoc.; E87(c), NASA; E87(b), W. Kaufmann/Photo Researchers; E88(tl), NASA; E88(tr), E88(c), E88(bl), E88(br), NASA/Photri; E89(t), NASA; E89(b), NASA/Photri; E90-E91(bg), Wendy Shattil, Bob Rozinski/Tom Stack & Assoc.; E91(l), NASA; E92-E93(bg), Greg Vaughn/Tom Stack & Assoc.; E94, Gerald & Buff Corsi/Tom Stack & Assoc.; E95, NASA.